THOU SHAL

How to Remember Everything in the Old Testament

I pray this may help you to remember all that's good & true or important to you!

[signature]

THOU SHALT REMEMBER

How to Remember Everything in the Old Testament

By David R. Larsen

ISBN: 1-55517-901-0
v.1

Published by Cedar Fort, Inc.
925 N. Main, Springville, Utah, 84663
www.cedarfort.com

Distributed by:

Cover design by Nicole Williams
Cover design © 2005 by Lyle Mortimer

Printed in the United States of America
10 9 8 7 6 5 4 3 2 1

Printed on acid-free paper

CONTENTS

ACKNOWLEDGMENTS

I want to acknowledge a few of the many people who have contributed to this book. First, I thank my wonderful parents, Howard and Josephine. Not only did they teach me to treasure up and develop a love for the scriptures, but also, through their examples, they helped me to see the value of retaining the scriptures "in remembrance" and applying them in my life.

I express appreciation for my dear wife, Maureen. She was supremely patient and typically supportive while I neglected her "honey-do" lists to pursue this more personally enjoyable project.

I also want to thank my children, David and Heidi—both

great writers in their own right—for reviewing my material and offering corrections, ideas, and encouragement.

I'd especially like to thank my friend Ron Nybo for his hours of selfless service, candid insights, cautions, and encouragement in reviewing and editing my many rough drafts. The A RECORD formula outlined in chapter 3 never would have been developed without his gentle prodding for an easier acronym.

I also want to express my gratitude to Lee Nelson of Cedar Fort for believing in the value and potential of this book and for his quick response and offer. I also thank Michael Morris and his staff for their hours of editing under intense pressure.

Thanks to my many friends and former students who were supportive when they could have been skeptical. Finally, thanks to my employer, Hill Air Force Base, for generously allowing me time off to complete this project.

INTRODUCTION

In this new age of technology, with televisions, computers, digital recorders, and so much more readily available to find and retrieve any information we might need, the one thing we may be neglecting is that marvelous God-given apparatus that exceeds them all—our brain. We may have become too content to let other people and things do the studying, the searching, and even some of the thinking and evaluating for us.

As a result, even while our brains are being increasingly enriched with sensory input, our memories, creativity, reasoning, communication, and other cognitive abilities may be atrophying in the wake of this increasing dependency.

We find good evidence that centuries ago our ancestors had much better memories and personal systems for remembering than most employ today. In Old Testament times, some people could recall and recite their family history back numerous generations. Victor Ludlow, one of the Church's premier Old Testament scholars, noted, "Rather than relying upon written records, the ancient Semites were trained to remember long passages. The development of their oral retention allowed them to pass on religious records, poetry, psalms, family histories, and other important information (*Isaiah: Prophet, Seer, and Poet*, 31–32).

Many Jews today can still recite significant amounts of the Torah, but unfortunately, memorization, as well as other memory skills, are becoming a lost art, primarily from disuse. Sadly, this seems to be the case even among the Latter-day Saints.

Of course, as with every good thing that does not get done, we have an excuse. We have technology. Why bother to memorize scriptures when we have them at our fingertips, literally! With today's laptop computers and, as if the scriptures weren't accessible enough, palm pilots, we can push a few buttons and pull the scriptures up on a screen.

But all of these aids to memory, or convenient crutches for recall, come with mixed blessings. They each carry a hazard. For as with any crutch, the more we do with them, the less we can do without them. The more we become dependent upon them, the less capable we become of performing these tasks on our own, unaided by gadgetry.

Unfortunately, these modern conveniences of the new information era have led to and perpetuated a type of sensory welfare system in which we may have become all too reliant upon others to do our studying and thinking for us; too reliant upon others to create vivid, memorable impressions; too reliant upon others to find, store, and retrieve the input needed for making important decisions; too reliant upon others to entertain us and to teach our children.

This book is not only about how to remember what you read

in the Old Testament but also about taking back control of our brains, of our own sensory input, and of our own thinking, evaluating, reasoning, and recall abilities. When we do this, we cease to be so reliant upon others and become better stewards of the gifts and agency God has granted us.

We take only one thing from this life—our memories. My desire is that this book will help you and your children expand your memories and treasure up the wisdom and insights of the Old Testament, so that you will not only have "an advantage in the world to come" (D&C 130:19) but also in this modern world as well.

1

REMEMBERING—THE FORGOTTEN KEY TO RIGHTEOUSNESS IN THE OLD TESTAMENT

Elder Neal A. Maxwell noted, "The scriptures constitute the moral memory of mankind . . . without which so many have 'suffered in ignorance' (Mosiah 1:3). Used effectively, the scriptures, as was done anciently, can actually enlarge 'the memory of this people,' emancipating them, in a sense, from the limitations of their own time."[1]

In the centuries before Christ, the collective memory of God's dealings with His children were available in only one source—the collection of books we now call the Old Testament. This was God's "guidebook" for His people in their earthly journeys. But even though these books are old, the counsel, wisdom, and revelations we find in these pages are as relevant today as they were back then.

Jesus noted that one of our primary purposes in life is to come to know God (see John 17:3). The Old Testament is of priceless value in that quest. It provides numerous insights into the nature of God through His various communications with the prophets and people. And, perhaps better than any other book, it provides profound insights into the nature of man. As we read about how our ancestors dealt with their difficulties, triumphs, and sorrows, we learn wisdom that can bless our lives and families.

The Apostle Paul noted that the holy scriptures (books of the Old Testament) "are able to make one wise unto salvation," that "they are profitable for doctrine, reproof, correction, and instruction in righteousness" (2 Timothy 3:15, 17). However, if you think about it, this can only be true if we are able to remember and apply the lessons contained therein. The Old Testament is a tremendous source of insight and wisdom, but in the final analysis, it is useless if like ancient Israel we forget this carefully recorded counsel from God.

Our ability to remember is not only a key to recalling and learning from the past but also a primary determinant of the quality of our present, as well as our future. Modern cognitive psychologists have proven the validity of Proverbs 23:7: "For as he thinketh in his heart, so *is* he."[2]

We know from numerous studies, particularly during the past thirty years, that what we remember, and therefore what we think about, is a primary determinant of our daily attitudes, our dominant feelings, our daily decisions, our personal behavior, and therefore, as E. D. Boardman observed, our "eternal destiny."[3]

How can we follow the counsel of God and keep His commandments if we can't remember what those commandments are? How can we apply the wisdom of Proverbs or feel the solace of Psalms if we can't remember what we read there? A careful reading of the scriptures reveals that a good memory is an essential key to righteous living.

This is a basic principle that God has been aware of from the beginning. Obviously, He knows our mortal tendency to forget, that the veil of forgetfulness has residual effects throughout our lives. He also knows that if we were not somehow reminded of important things over and over again, we would not remember them and they would have limited effect on our lives during this period of mortal probation. Therefore, from Adam on down, God has repeatedly counseled His people to remember certain things and even provided visual aids to help us remember. In Deuteronomy alone we read, "thou shalt remember" or "thou shalt not forget" no less than seven times. Additionally, there are more than two hundred twelve references to remembering and at least sixty-six warnings to "not forget" in the Old Testament.

While in the wilderness, the children of Israel learned that "man doth not live by bread alone, but by every word which proceedeth out of the mouth of the Lord" (Deuteronomy 8:3).

But what if we forget those words? The Old Testament graphically describes the consequences. One of the most important lessons the scriptures teach is the importance of remembering. Over and over again, we see how easily men can forget the counsel of their God, even when their salvation depends on remembering and sad consequences follow forgetting.

One of the primary problems mentioned in the Bible, and the initial cause of the downfall of Israel, was the tendency to forget. The Lord, therefore, warned them early on to "take heed to thyself, and keep thy soul diligently, lest thou *forget* the things which thine eyes have seen, and lest they depart from thy heart all the days of thy life: but teach them thy sons, and thy sons' sons" (Deuteronomy 4:9; emphasis added).

We also read, "Take heed unto yourselves, lest ye *forget* the covenant of the Lord your God, which he made with you, and make you a graven image, or the likeness of any thing, which the Lord thy God hath forbidden thee" (Deuteronomy 4:23; emphasis added).

But as David later lamented, "Our fathers understood not thy wonders in Egypt; they *remembered* not the multitude of thy mercies; but provoked him at the sea, even at the Red sea" (Psalm 106:7; emphasis added). And as a result, we know many of them turned from their God and Savior and, because of their forgetfulness, were made to wander in the desert forty years.

While the children of Israel were wandering, Moses repeatedly decreed, "And thou shalt *remember* that thou wast a bondman in the land of Egypt, and the Lord thy God redeemed thee" (Deuteronomy 15:15; emphasis added; see also Deuteronomy 16:12; 24:18, 22).

Then again to calm their fears before entering the promised land, and before his final departure, Moses commanded the Israelites, "Thou shalt not be afraid of them: but shalt well *remember* what the Lord thy God did unto Pharaoh, and unto all Egypt" (Deuteronomy 7:18; emphasis added).

And again, "And thou shalt *remember* all the way which the Lord thy God led thee these forty years in the wilderness, to humble thee, and to prove thee, to know what was in thine heart, whether thou wouldest keep his commandments, or no" (Deuteronomy 8:2; emphasis added).

And finally, "Thou shalt *remember* the Lord thy God: for it is he that giveth thee power to get wealth, that he may establish his covenant which he sware unto thy fathers, as it is this day" (Deuteronomy 8:18; emphasis added).

Moreover, Moses' final warnings focused on the importance of not forgetting: "And it shall be, if thou do at all *forget* the Lord thy God, and walk after other gods, and serve them, and worship them, I testify against you this day that ye shall surely perish" (Deuteronomy 8:19; emphasis added; see also 2 Kings 17:38).

Unfortunately, despite this counsel, as later prophets testified, "the children of Israel *remembered not* the Lord their God, who had delivered them out of the hands of all their enemies on every side" (Judges 8:34; emphasis added). As a result, the next generation "knew not the Lord, nor yet the works which he had done for Israel" (Judges 2:10). As a result, their decisions and behavior deteriorated into apostasy.

In response, the Lord himself lamented: "Can a maid *forget* her ornaments, or a bride her attire? Yet my people *have forgotten* me days without number" (Jeremiah 2:32; emphasis added). So finally, the Lord declared their fate.

In Ezekiel, the Lord said, "Because thou hast not *remembered* the days of thy youth, but hast fretted me in all these things; behold, therefore I also will recompense thy way upon thine head, saith the Lord God" (vv. 22, 43; emphasis added).

And because they had forgotten Him, in His wrath He declared what their fathers had feared the most[4]—that He would *forget* them. "Therefore, behold, I, even I, will utterly *forget* you, and I will forsake you, and the city that I gave you and your fathers, and cast you out of my presence" (Jeremiah 23:39; emphasis added).

"My people are destroyed for lack of knowledge: because thou hast rejected knowledge, I will also reject thee, that thou shalt be no priest to me: seeing thou hast *forgotten* the law of thy God, I will also *forget* thy children" (Hosea 4:6; emphasis added).

Remembering—the First Step in the Repentance Process

Just as forgetting leads to wandering and apostasy, the Bible testifies that remembering is a first step leading to repentance and regaining favor with the Lord. Peter understood this when he wrote, "I think it meet, as long as I am in this tabernacle, to stir you up by putting you *in remembrance*" (2 Peter 1:13; emphasis added).

Even so Jeremiah counseled Israel, "Ye that have escaped the sword, go away, stand not still: *remember* the Lord afar off, and let Jerusalem come into your mind" (Jeremiah 51:50; emphasis added).

We know that sorrow for sin is among the first steps of repentance, but how could Israel feel that sorrow if they did not remember what they had done wrong? So the Lord declared, "Then thou shalt *remember* thy ways, and be ashamed. . . . And

5

there shall ye *remember* your ways, and all your doings, wherein ye have been defiled; and ye shall lothe yourselves in your own sight for all your evils that ye have committed (Ezekiel 16:61; 20:43; emphasis added).

Even though they had forgotten Him, the Lord says He will still remember His promises and extend His mercies, that they might remember and be ashamed. "And I will establish my covenant with thee; and thou shalt know that I am the Lord: That thou mayest *remember*, and be confounded" (Ezekiel 16:63; emphasis added).

"And I will sow them among the people: and they shall *remember* me in far countries; and they shall live with their children, and turn again" (Zechariah 10:9; emphasis added).

Once the children of Israel finally did remember, King David believed "all the ends of the world . . . all the kindreds of the nations" would "turn unto the Lord" and worship before him. And "they shall abundantly utter the memory of thy great goodness, and shall sing of thy righteousness" (Psalm 22:27; 145:7).

King David's Lapse in Memory

After Israel's early episodes of forgetfulness, and subsequent fall from grace, later Old Testament writers were adamant about the importance of remembering, especially if they themselves had suffered from a lapse in memory. The once-faithful King David is a prolific example. In his Psalms, he affirms more than seven times his willingness to now remember. He also reminds his readers to "remember [the Lord and] his marvelous works that he hath done; his wonders, and the judgments of his mouth" (Psalm 105:5), and to "keep his covenant" and follow his commandments (Psalm 103:18). He then pleads over and over with the Lord to remember, and have mercy on him (see Psalm 25:6–7; 74:2; 106:4; 137:6–7) and not remember his sins (Psalm 25:7; 79:8). Finally, King David graphically and poignantly declares, "If I do not remember thee, let my tongue cleave to the roof of my mouth" (Psalm 137:6).

Surely, King David understood the importance of remembering. Unfortunately he had to learn that, or be reminded of it, the hard way by a prophet of God (2 Samuel 12:7–10). Thankfully, the Old Testament prophets illustrate easier ways to help us remember.

The Lord Helps His People Remember

Since God "hath made his wonderful works to be remembered" and since He realizes His children's tendency to forgetfulness and because "the Lord is gracious and full of compassion" (Psalm 111:4), He provided His prophets and people with various signs, symbols, types, names, and other memory aids.

For example, He had an angel teach Adam about animal sacrifices to help Adam and his family remember that one day He, the Lord, would provide a savior, whose sacrifice would allow Adam and his posterity to once again return to the presence of God (see Moses 5:6–7). After the flood, God gave a rainbow. "And the bow shall be in the cloud; and I will look upon it, that I may *remember* the everlasting covenant between God and every living creature of all flesh that is upon the earth" (Genesis 9:15–16; emphasis added).

After Israel left Egypt, God instituted the Passover with bitter herbs and unleavened bread to remind His children of the bitterness of their bondage and their haste in fleeing from captivity in Egypt (see Exodus 13:3; Deuteronomy 16:3), as well as His mercy in sparing them from the Egyptian plagues and freeing them from bondage (see Exodus 12:11, 27).

And since the children of Israel continued to have a hard time remembering, the Lord had them write down His words and "bind them for a sign upon thine hand, and . . . as frontlets between thine eyes." He also required them to wear a fringe on their garments "that ye may look upon it, and *remember* all the commandments of the Lord, and do them." Additionally, they were commanded to "write them upon the posts of thy house, and on thy gates . . . *lest they forget* the Lord, which brought thee forth out of the land of Egypt, from the house of bondage" (Deuteronomy 6:8; 6:9; Numbers 15:39; emphasis added).

Later the ordinance of baptism was instituted to help the Israelites remember that their sins could be washed away in the blood of Christ (see 1 Corinthians 11: 24–25) and that the old man of sin was to be buried and born again unto life eternal through the Atonement of Christ (see Romans 6:6).

God appointed priests and teachers "that thereby they [the people] might hear and know the commandments of God, and to stir them up *in remembrance* of the oath which they had made" (Mosiah 6:3; emphasis added; see also Alma 4:19).

And of course, one of the Lord's methods for reminding His children of their baptismal covenants is through the sacrament and associated prayers. "And he took bread, and gave thanks, and brake *it,* and gave unto them, saying, This is my body which is given for you: this do *in remembrance* of me" (Luke 22:19; emphasis added).

And, "After the same manner also he took the cup, when he had supped, saying, This cup is the new testament in my blood: this do ye, as oft as ye drink it, *in remembrance* of me (1 Corinthians 11:25; emphasis added). How could anyone who loves the Lord commit a sin, if at the same time they were remembering Him and His sacrifice for them?

Down through the centuries God has also directed men, usually His prophets, to write His words on parchment or sticks, goat skins, and metal plates in order that they might be remembered (see Ezekiel 37:16; 1 Nephi 19:3; Mormon 1:4).

Of course, the written word is an important aid to memory. As King Benjamin notes, "For it were not possible that our father, Lehi, could have remembered all these things [from the Old Testament], to have taught them to his children, except it were for the help of these plates" (Mosiah 1:4).

Benjamin continued by saying, "My sons, I would that ye should remember that were it not for these plates, which contain these records and these commandments, we must have suffered in ignorance, even at this present time, not knowing the mysteries of God" (Mosiah 1:3).

The great Old Testament scholar Victor Ludlow has noted, "The ancient poets, prophets, writers, and scribes would assist their followers by organizing their material into an easily remembered form. Old Testament authors often used key phrases or words as verbal flags to alert the listener to important passages that would be coming up shortly in their presentation. They also used memory devices or patterns that made the poems easy to remember and still allowed the composer spontaneity of expression."[5]

Ludlow notes the most common of these patterns in Hebrew poetry was parallelism.[6] Chiasmus, a self-repeating literary design used extensively in the Book of Mormon, was one of the more advanced examples of this ancient poetic memory aid.[7] God also inspired His prophets and other Old Testament writers to use metaphors and various other literary devices or reiterations to help clarify, reinforce, and remind them of the concepts being taught.

The Psalms of David were written in poetic style to help bring them to remembrance. The book of Ezekiel uses chiasmus extensively to remind ancient Israel that the day would come when Israel would remember her evil ways and her covenants with the Lord. The book of Hosea appears to be another grand metaphor or reminder of the Lord's infinite love and patience in dealing with His wayward wife Israel.

Harsher Reminders

Of course, the Lord has other less desirable ways to help us remember. These methods include famine, pestilence, plagues, enemies, and other afflictions. The Lord has warned His people that if they cannot remember His words and follow them, He is willing to "stir them up to remembrance" through one or more of these means (see Joshua 23:13; Judges 2:20–22; 2 Nephi 5:25;

Lamentations 1:5; Mosiah 1:17; 9:3, 17; Alma 4:3; I Kings 8:35, 37; Helaman 11:4, 34; 12:3).

These memory helps, however, had some obviously negative side effects. Therefore, the Israelites used a variety of other memory cues, or links, to help them remember. In other words, by remembering one fact, another fact would be brought to mind. For example, the bitter herbs and unleavened bread brought to mind their bondage and the mercy of the Lord in delivering them. Their lambs and sacrifices were linked to "the Lamb of God, who taketh away the sins of the world" (Alma 7:14). The ritual of the scapegoat reminded them that their sins could be forgiven. The dove, olive branch, and oil were symbols of peace, purity, healing, and the Holy Ghost. Figs were associated with fertility—and the forbidden fruit, which suggests sin and the Fall of man. Incense reminded them of their prayers ascending to God. Salt was a symbol of purity and preservation from corruption. Water symbolized cleansing, sanctification, and revelation.[8]

Numbers also had associated meanings. The number 7 symbolized wholeness and spiritual perfection. In Egypt, it referred to eternal life. The number 12 was not only the number of the tribes of Israel but also a symbol for the priesthood and power to govern, while 13 was even then an evil omen.

Without some types of memory aids, we are prone, like Tevye in *The Fiddler on the Roof*, to misquote scripture. "As the good book says," Tevye declared, "if a man has a chicken . . ." And then we might exclaim, as he did, in frustration, "Well, it says something about a chicken somewhere."

Personal Application

Personally I am very aware of the value of a good memory and understanding of the scriptures. There have been many times in my life that I have failed to do or say important things. On occasion, these have been things that I really wanted to do or say, but I simply forgot, or at least couldn't remember at the most opportune times. Some of this was just lack of adequate organization, clear priorities, or failure to post or look at reminders. However, at other times I was simply unable to recall information or ideas I had previously read or learned.

Fortunately, I've found a cure for that ailment. In this book, I share what I've learned on how to become better organized mentally, how to create mental reminders and other memory aids, and how to recall or locate important concepts or ideas from the scriptures, particularly the Old Testament, when we need them.

Practical Applications

There are many practical daily applications and advantages to being able to recall at will what is contained in the scriptures, or locate important counsel at opportune times. This ability can be invaluable in our roles as parents, teachers, and missionaries in simply making daily decisions and in keeping our mind, mood, and life in balance.

As parents we have a responsibility to teach our children the ways and wisdom of the Lord. To paraphrase, Proverbs 22:6 notes that if we can train up our children in the ways they should go, when they are older, they will not depart from those ways. In this responsibility, we are reminded of Timothy's counsel that "all scripture is . . . profitable for doctrine, for reproof, for correction, for instruction in righteousness" (2 Timothy 3:16). The Old Testament does not have many long sermons, but it is full of great stories that teach sound principles and moral courage. And stories are what children love to hear. Reading Bible stories to children at bedtime is a great idea, but being able to relate a relevant story on the spot, as we encounter teaching moments throughout the day, can be of tremendous additional value.

When I was growing up, both of my parents knew the gospel and the scriptures, and they shared that knowledge with us from time to time in our daily work. My mother would tell us stories from her childhood of how her prayers were answered, and she'd share the relevant scriptures that inspired her. By the time I was twelve, I knew Proverbs 3:5 by heart: "Trust in the Lord with all thine heart, lean not unto thine own understanding, but in all thy ways acknowledge him and he will direct thy paths."

Although I had never actually read that scripture, I learned and absorbed it into memory simply from hearing my mother repeat it over and over throughout my early years, along with her many faith-promoting stories.

My father didn't share as many personal stories, but he knew stories from Bible. So as we went about our daily tasks on the farm, my father would share these various stories and other verses from the scriptures. As I grew older, and as needed, he shared other wise sayings or quotes from memory. And again, there are some that I don't recall ever reading at that age. I just knew them from hearing my father recite them.

So from my parents, I learned the stories of the Old Testament. I particularly enjoyed the story of young David (my namesake) and his faith as he faced a lion, a bear, and finally Goliath. I even remember my father helping me to fashion a slingshot. Though I was never very good with it, it helped me to vividly imagine David and his close encounters.

This upbringing helped me and my siblings understand the value of committing scriptures and other wisdom to memory. This proved extremely valuable to me as I served a mission and later served as a chaplain in the military. In fact, it has been most helpful to me throughout my life as a teacher, Church leader, husband, father, and even grandfather.

In the next nine chapters, I'll share with you the basic principles, as well as advanced methods, for scripture memory mastery. You will learn how to remember anything you ever wanted to from the Old Testament, as well as who said what and where. In chapter 10, we'll discuss ways to keep your memory sharp and clear even into old age. In chapter 11, you will learn how an application of these principles can help you overcome temptations, bad habits, absentmindedness, and even addictions.

Finally in chapter 12, you will learn about the most powerful memory aid on earth and how you can access and use this

valuable gift to bless not only your life but others' lives as well.
So, let's get started!

Notes

1. Neal A. Maxwell, *Sermons Not Spoken*, 4.

2. Except now we know that thinking takes place primarily in the brain.

3. E. D. Boardman, in Jack M. Lyon, et al., *Best-Loved Poems of the LDS People*, 18.

4. Numerous pleadings are recorded from various prophets, kings, and others in Israel that the Lord not forget them (see 1 Samuel 1:11; Nehemiah 13:14; Jeremiah 15:15, 22; Psalm 13:1; Lamentations 5:20). That was apparently one of the greatest fears of the ancient faithful.

5. Victor L. Ludlow, *Isaiah: Prophet, Seer, and Poet*, 31–32.

6. Ibid.

7. See John W. Welch, *Chiasmus in Antiquity*.

8. For a great review of the names, symbols, and types used in the Old Testament and other scriptures, see Alonzo Gaskill, *The Lost Language of Symbolism*.

2

THE ANATOMY OF A
GREAT MEMORY

You may want to dive right into discovering new and better ways to enhance your memory. However, before we jump into the Seven Habits of Highly Effective Learners—and the associated strategies and techniques for memory enhancement—it seems prudent to take a few pages to review what makes a good memory and why our memories sometimes fail us.

Basically, there are two different aspects to memory. The first I will call *natural memory*. This organic part of memory can be thought of as the soil or physiology of our mind. It includes the gray matter, the neurons, neurotransmitters, and other structures that make up the brain and its intricate communication systems.

The second aspect of memory can be referred to as our *memory processes*. These are the developed or trained aspects of our memory; those procedures, strategies, and techniques that we employ, consciously or automatically, to remember things better and get the most out of our *natural memory*.

In this book, we will focus primarily on improving our memory processes. However, it's essential to have some understanding of both because they are inextricably tied together. In chapter 10, we will discuss ways that you can also optimize your natural memory.

If our natural memory is not working well, these suggested strategies for memory enhancement won't work well either. This would be like having a new eight-cylinder truck with power steering and four-wheel drive capacity that can barely make it out of the garage because only four of the cylinders are firing.

Conversely, even if our brain were running close to optimum naturally, if it is not organized, or if we are not employing strategies to optimize its potential, we will continue to operate well below our capacity. That would be like having a V-8 engine with lots of power but only two gears to operate in. We will get much farther faster and be able to accomplish much more with our memory if we can improve both aspects of memory.

Basically, the causes of most memory problems can be broken down into the following four related categories: Natural (physiology), Processes, Storage, and Retrieval. These categories can be diagrammed as follows:

Natural Storage	Storage Processes
Natural Retrieval	Retrieval Processes

Even though these functions have been placed into distinct categories, it's important to keep in mind that each function interacts with and, to some extent, is dependent upon the others for optimal functioning or total recall ability.

In order for our natural brain physiology to function properly for effective storage and retrieval, we need five things:

1. **Healthy cerebral cellular structures**—These structures include neurons, dendrites, axons, and cell membranes. If these membranes are not healthy, the necessary nutrients will not be able to pass through to supply the vital chemistry needed for memory transmission.

2. **Neurotransmitters**—We're talking specifically about acetylcholine, dopamine, and norepinephrine. These are the chemical messengers of the brain, responsible for alertness, as well as encoding, transferring, storing, and retrieving memories.

3. **Good nutrition**—This includes a variety of proteins, vitamins, minerals, lipids or essential fatty acids (EFA), and carbohydrates. These are the building blocks and the fuel of the brain. They work together to create neurotransmitters and maintain cell walls and other brain structures. Although it accounts for only 2 percent of our body weight, our brain burns 20–30 percent of the body's total available energy and requires a wide variety of nutrients.

4. **Plenty of oxygen**—The brain's various activities require a great deal of oxygen. We all know that when totally deprived of oxygen, brain cells can die within minutes. Less known is the fact that even a reduced consumption of oxygen, over time, can cause significant memory problems.

5. **An effective circulatory system**—Since the brain cannot store the nutrients, calories, and oxygen it needs, it must constantly rely on a healthy delivery system. This may be thought of as the Achilles heel of memory. Clogged arteries or an otherwise sluggish circulatory system can deprive the brain of the essential oxygen and other nutrients it needs to synthesize neurotransmitters and function properly. This is why exercise is so important for a healthy mind and memory

For our memories to function at an optimal level, all of the above noted elements need to be performing their own proper function and working in concert with each other. In addition, they should not be inhibited by any other harmful substances, including drugs or medications.[1] If any one of these elements is missing or seriously depleted, or if other substances are inhibiting proper function, it will manifest itself in some type of cognitive or mental deficit, from poor concentration and confusion to a total loss of consciousness and severe brain damage. Even a low-grade problem, in one or more of these areas over time, can result in memory storage or retrieval problems. In short, people thus afflicted simply won't be able to recall what they want to, when they want to, even though they feel they ought to be able to.

There are many reasons why a person might experience problems with their natural memory physiology. The most common are vascular or circulatory problems. Therefore, it is always best to *consult your physician* or a neurologist if you are experiencing a significant decline in memory to determine the most likely cause. Otherwise you could end up wasting a lot of time and money pursuing blind alleys when the light, in fact, lies at the end of another path.

The nutrients (described in chapter 10) and strategies (described in chapters 3–9) in this book can prove useful in preventing or dealing with a wide variety of memory problems, but the more you know about your specific needs, the better you and your doctor will be able to develop a program that is effective for you.

Why We Can't Recall All We Read

The two basic processes of memory are *storage* and *retrieval*. Most of us feel that we have a problem with retrieval. We just can't recall or remember what was read, said, or done. However, in reality the most common and correctable problems that prevent good recall are not in retrieval so much as in the way we store, or more correctly, do *not* store information. This is especially true as we grow older.

When most people talk of short-term memory, they are

referring to the ability to remember events of the past day or hour. However, when neurologists or cognitive psychologists talk of short-term memory, they are referring to a much shorter time period—the time immediately after information is received, or the period during which information either is or is not transferred into (recent) long-term memory.

Short-term or temporary memory, as it is sometimes called, generally lasts only a few seconds, or at most a minute or two. For example, when someone tells you their phone number, short term is the time between when you first hear the number and when you write it down or use it in making a call.

For example, if you were to look up a seven-digit phone number then close the book, that number would usually stay in your head long enough for you to dial it, especially if you were repeating it to yourself over and over. However, if someone interrupted this process to ask for directions, the number would be lost in the short time it would take to provide those directions. Why? Because, unless you had, in that brief moment, activated some procedure for long-term storage, the number would not have been adequately recorded. This is the case for most of us. No doubt you have experienced this in the past.

The same thing tends to happen when we are introduced to more than one person at a time, or when we are reading. Our temporary memory usually does not retain information for an extended period, especially if it shifts focus to something else in the meantime. So if an interruption occurs before the number, name, or verse can be adequately stored in long-term memory, then for all practical purposes on earth,[2] it's gone for good, and you have to go back to the source to retrieve it. You cannot draw it out of your memory, no matter how hard you try, if it was never adequately stored there in the first place.

As noted, inadequate storage—getting information from short-term or temporary memory into longer-term or more permanent memory—is the most common cause of memory problems, for young and old alike.

Above I described how interruptions or distractions can

inhibit the adequate recording of memories. However, in reading the Old Testament you are likely to encounter a slightly different problem. This is technically referred to as *displacement.*

As we read, new information tends to displace previously read information in short-term memory. Therefore, if we want to be able to remember what we have read, we must learn how to make those transfers from temporary to longer term memory as efficiently and impressively as possible to avoid loss through fading, displacement, or other distractions. In later chapters, I will share more specific methods for accomplishing this; the following is only a quick preview.

Since we are constantly being interrupted with new information coming in on top of previous inputs, you may be wondering how we manage to remember anything! Well, we actually don't remember most things we hear; we are able to recall more of what we see. And when we are able to recall what we have read, it's usually because we have imagined or visualized what we were reading as we read about it. Most people can commit a picture to memory much faster and more indelibly than any written description of that picture.

This is pretty much an unconscious process. However, if we do not create those visual images with enough clarity and power to make a deep sensory impression, it's unlikely the information will be adequately stored in long-term memory. So it will not be available for recollection or retrieval at any future point in time.

Fortunately, sages and scholars through the ages have developed various ways to consciously facilitate this process of transferring or storing information. By utilizing these methods, you will be able to store wisdom and insights from the Old Testament with such clarity and power that they will be available for retrieval and use days, weeks, months, and even years later.

Here's an example. I was teaching a communications class and asked one of my students what her husband's name was. She told me and I went on with the point I was trying to make. I then tried to refer back to her husband, but his name was not there. Somewhat embarrassed, I had to ask his name again. "I guess you didn't get it transferred from short to long-term memory," she said.

"You are right!" I said. "How do you know about that?"

"Well," she replied, "I was in your memory class last spring."

"Yes, I thought you looked familiar," I responded. Fortunately, the memory class had been large and was only one session. This gave me a better excuse for not having remembered her in that setting.

"Remember Lois Lane?" she asked.

"Yes, I do," I replied. Lois was the name of one of the class members. We had used an association technique (described in chapter 7), pairing qualities of this Lois with Lois Lane, Superman's girlfriend, to burn her name into our brains.

The point is that we could both still remember that name and person after several months, with no rehearsal in between. However, since I had not applied any of these procedures to remembering her husband's name, it had slipped from my memory, even though she had mentioned it only minutes before.

Before I proceed, you should know, in case you haven't already detected it, that I am not an Albert Einstein or a Hugh Nibley. I do not have an exceptional memory, although I have demonstrated what might be considered exceptional memory feats. I believe that I have an average natural memory. I have had my share of problems remembering things, especially names. But fortunately, I recognized this weakness early and so have sought long and hard to overcome it.

I have attended various university courses on memory. I own numerous books and tapes on the subject. The last course I sent back for a refund. The company had advertised "new and dramatic insights," but there was nothing new to me. At that point I realized that I knew all of this stuff and that I needed to share what I knew. (See the notes and references at the end of the chapters in this book for a list of excellent, up-to-date sources on the subject.)

I have taught this subject off and on for the past fifteen years in various settings. I wouldn't call myself an expert, but I think that I have learned a few things in the process of helping myself and others. So what was once a weakness, with the help of the Lord and other true experts, has become a strength (see Ether 12:27). I hope that this knowledge can be of value to you and yours to strengthen your ability to remember, especially what you read in your studies of the Old Testament.

I want to warn you, however. Although the following methods work amazingly well to improve memory and recall, these principles and techniques will not be effective in helping you remember important information from the Old Testament *unless* you apply and practice them. You must learn and consistently apply, consciously or unconsciously, these principles when you study the Old Testament if you are to enjoy dramatically enhanced recall ability of that material. If you do, I promise that you will.

Notes

1. A variety of prescription drugs may negatively affect memory. If you suspect such an effect, discuss it with your doctor. Some of the nutrients noted in chapter 10 may help to counteract adverse effects, but if you are on any type of prescription medication, it's wise to consult with your doctor before taking these.

2. Evidence in the scriptures and near-death studies suggest that when people are near death, some experience nearly total recall of past events in rich, sensory detail (see chapters 5 and 6).

3

THE SEVEN HABITS OF HIGHLY EFFECTIVE LEARNERS

In his blockbuster book *The Seven Habits of Highly Effective People,* Stephen Covey talks about seven behaviors that, if consistently practiced, will lead to success in business and life. Moreover, these seven habits are built upon foundational principles for effective personal development and interpersonal relations.[1]

Principles serve a critical purpose in our lives. When asked how he governed his people, Joseph Smith stated, "I teach them correct principles and they govern themselves."[2] Similarly, it appears that most people who have outstanding recall abilities, either consciously or unconsciously, apply what I call the seven habits of highly effective learners. These habits are also built upon foundational principles, principles that govern the storage and retrieval of information in the brain.

Most people understand what a habit is, but fewer people understand the nature and value of principles. So let's review a few definitions. A *principle* is defined in the dictionary as a fundamental truth or law, as the basis of reasoning and action, or a law of nature or science.

This definition calls to mind D&C 130:21, which states, "And when we obtain any blessing from God, it is by obedience to that law upon which it is predicated."

Therefore, if we want to obtain a good memory, and effectively recall insights and lessons when needed from the Old Testament, it would be wise to first obtain a clear understanding of the laws or principles upon which a good memory, or effective storage and retrieval, is based. Then it would serve us well to develop habits that are in line with those principles.

In behavioral science, however, a *principle* is defined a bit differently; it is referred to as a statement about the relationship between two variables. A variable is something that varies, either increases or decreases, getting stronger or weaker.

Typically, this statement describes how a change in one of these variables (an action or behavior) affects another variable (result). In other words, how a change in A affects B. For example, one of the most basic principles of memory relates the act of rehearsal-to-recall ability. This principle can be stated as follows: The more frequently and actively a person rehearses information, the greater that person's ability to remember that information when needed. From this, we can see that, as the dictionary suggests, statements of principle reflect basic underlying laws of nature—in this case human nature, and more specifically the nature of how our memories work and are governed.

One of the nice things about principles, and why I genuinely enjoyed studying about them in graduate school, is that once you understand the principles that govern behaviors or interactions in a given field, it's easier to determine appropriate specific behaviors in that area. Moreover, underlying principles can be applied in many different settings and used to develop various methods or techniques that would be effective in novel situations or uncharted territory.

For example, the Rehearsal Principle stated above can be applied to strengthening recall ability of information from almost any source in almost any area of study, including science, religion, and human relations.

The discussion above might seem a bit esoteric for our purposes. After all, this is not a college course, and it is certainly not meant to be a science project. Rather, I want to provide a practical guide that almost anyone could benefit from. Hopefully, you will soon see how this information relates to making the concepts, principles, habits, methods, and techniques outlined in this book more useful for you.

So now that you better understand what principles are, why they are important, and how they can relate to behaviors and habits, let's explore some specific principles and related habits that apply to improving our memories. Then we will apply these principles more specifically to remembering passages, stories, and wisdom from he Old Testament. If you learn and apply these principles well, you will be amazed at how much more effective you will be in governing your memory and getting it to produce for you.

Most of the basic principles for improving memory processes can be summed up with the acronym A RECORD. So if you want to remember something, you simply have to make A RECORD. Acronyms (using the first letter of the words you want to remember to form another word that will help remind you of each of the other words) are one of many methods[3] we will review to help facilitate recall. Here are the memory-enhancing principles and habits in the A RECORD formula.

The first **A** stands for *attention*. Often when we forget a verse of scripture or other piece of information, it is not a problem with our memory or retrieval system so much as we simply didn't pay close enough *attention* when the information was presented.

Despite what you may have heard about recall under hypnosis, or subliminal learning, our brain simply does not effectively store everything that goes on around us or that passes through our field of vision or within earshot.

In order to remember something specific, we must first focus our attention on that specific thing, and then we must get involved with that information. The following are all principles of involvement, which is an extension of the attention principle. Generally, we can only store for long-term retrieval those things that we pay close attention to. That being said, pay close attention to the following statements:

The Attention Principle: The more attention we pay to whatever we see or hear, the easier it will be to remember.

The Attention Habit: Pay close attention to, and get involved with, those things that you wish to remember.

The first **R** in RECORD stands for *relate*. Some experts feel this is the real key to effective storage and retrieval. As we read or hear new information, it generally sticks best when we can relate or associate it in a memorable way with something that we already know. This is one reason that older individuals sometimes do better at retaining new information than younger people. Older minds have more information and experiences to which they can tie or associate new information. This causes new information to be more meaningful, which in turn causes them to pay better attention and become more involved in developing an image or related association that will stick in long-term memory.

Most memory training methods, strategies, or techniques are simply ways people have developed to help them relate new information to more familiar knowledge. This key process is usually done with vivid, memorable picture associations, enabling us to better recall things that are new. In chapter 5, we will see a variety of methods for relating, or making vivid associations, to help us recall not only the teachings of the Old Testament but also who taught them and where they can be found.

The Relate Principle: The more we can relate new information to easily recalled information, the easier it will be to remember the new information.

The Relate Habit: Relate new information in concrete, easily envisioned ways to past familiar, easily recalled information.

The **E** in this formula stands for *envision*. Most people have better visual memories than auditory. We are able to remember events, concepts, and ideas better if we can see, picture, or visualize them, instead of only reading or hearing about them.

For example, most of us tend to remember pictures of a scene better than verbal descriptions of a scene. We tend to remember things we read better than things we hear, especially if a picture, diagram, or other graphic visual aid is included. The Envision Principle and the associated habit to be formed can be stated as follows:

The Envision Principle: The more vividly we can envision, or picture in our imagination, what we read or hear, the easier it will be to remember when needed.

The Envision Habit: Envision or picture what you wish to remember with as much sensory rich detail and as vividly as you can.

The **C** stands for *concrete*. Concrete objects, or things, are much easier to visualize, and thus remember, than are abstract concepts or ideas. So you may find it helpful to select objects to represent ideas. For example, honor is a concept or idea that is not easily visualized. Therefore, to represent *honor*, you may want to visualize a sword or shield, which might represent an "I'm willing to fight for your honor" type of feeling. For love, you might envision a heart; for honesty, you might imagine honest Abe Lincoln.

For this reason, in our language we use alphabetic symbols and words to represent sounds and concepts, and computer systems use icons or pictures to represent programs. This makes it easier to identify the program and recall the needed information. For most of us, our natural memories are fairly good. As with computers, we simply need a concrete clue, hint, or symbol to remind us and enable us to access and pull up the fuller memory. The associated principle and habit here are:

The Concrete Principle: Concrete visible objects are pictured and remembered more easily than less tangible concepts or ideas.

The Concrete Habit: Picture concrete objects or symbols to represent less tangible concepts or ideas.

The **O** stands for *organize* or to put in order. In the Doctrine and Covenants, we are told to "organize yourselves" (109:4). If we want a good memory, we also need to follow that counsel. Good memories are organized memories. Paul taught that "God is not the author of confusion" (1 Corinthians 14:33). Nor should we be in the things we want to commit to memory.

Like any file or retrieval system, if you want to find what you want when you want it, you need to store it in an organized manner in the first place. Order makes access and retrieval much easier. Of course, information can be organized in a variety of ways, including sequentially, by date or time; spatially, by location; numerically; or logically by category, to name just a few. (In chapter 7, we will see yet another way to organize our memories.)

The reason I can communicate with you in writing is because we both share the same orderly, concrete writing system. As with all writing systems, this system essentially organizes marks, which would otherwise be meaningless, into a mutually accepted and orderly strategy of symbols. Because we both give the same meaning to the same symbols and sounds, we are able to communicate and understand each other. Without this shared understanding, there would be confusion and chaos. The biblical name for it was Babel for the babble that ensued.

I remember trying to order food once in Paris using my best

English and Spanish. It was not a pleasant experience. As I recall I wanted a sandwich. What I got was French onion soup. Organization, and in that case an organized common language of symbols is essential to finding what you want.

Many chapters in the Old Testament are organized into carefully crafted poetry or chiasmus. These are based on parallelism, a method of "thought-rhythm" or reiteration. In these literary forms, ideas are repeated or reiterated, often with different words having similar meanings, or synonyms. One of the purposes of this, as Brother Ludlow noted, was to help the reader better understand and remember the concepts being taught.

I've tried to use a similar structure of reiteration with some concepts in this book, albeit not so poetic, but for the same reason. The important thing, however, is not so much how a message is organized—although it may help to know that—as that you organize a message in your mind in a way that is meaningful and logical for you. When you do, you will remember the message better.

The Organization Principle can be stated as follows:

The Organize Principle: The more we organize information in ways that are meaningful to us, the easier it will be for us to remember.

The Organize Habit: Organize what you wish to remember in ways that are meaningful to and memorable for you.

The second **R** stands for *repeat, rehearse,* or *reiterate.* Repetition is considered to be the mother of memory. Perhaps that is why the Hebrews, particularly David and Solomon, used it so often in their writings. However, I prefer to use the verb *rehearse* in this formula because it suggests a more involved, active, and dynamic process. Review or rehearsal sessions ideally should be set up within a few minutes of learning a new piece of information, then again within the hour, after a few hours, the next day, a few days later, and then finally a week later and at regular intervals as needed thereafter.

Spaced rehearsal is the key to long-term storage and recall. The Lord uses this principle in the Church. We are to attend meetings regularly, partake of the sacrament often, and study over and over the same gospel principles. In doing so, the Lord's teachings become more deeply ingrained in our brain and behavior, so we remember to apply them in our daily lives when needed.

There is a principle in educational and behavioral psychology called overlearning. Studies related to this suggest that the more we overlearn a process or information, the easier it is to access and apply. Perhaps that is what the Lord is trying to do with us through the various church programs. He wants us to learn the gospel so well that application becomes automatic. This Rehearsal Principle has already been stated as follows:

The Rehearsal Principle: The more frequently and actively we rehearse information, the greater our ability to remember that information when needed.

The Rehearsal Habit: Actively rehearse what you have learned at regular intervals as needed.

One way to rehearse and better remember any new information is to fold a regular piece of notebook paper down the middle. On the outside fold, write questions about the material you want to recall. On the inside, write the answers. Then during review sessions, look at the questions and see if you can recall the answers. If you have difficulty recalling any of the answers, you may want to review the above-noted principles for insights into what you could do differently. Then, using A RECORD as a guide and the ideas in chapter 4, develop a way to impress that information more vividly into your memory. It's also helpful to make a note of your memory clues or cues on the opposite side of the inner fold.

The **D** is for *deliver.* We could call this the "deliver paradox." After you receive and record new information, if you really want to retain it you've got to give it away. Deliver a lesson or sermon on it, or otherwise share[4] this information with others, perhaps your spouse, your children, friends, fellow class members, neighbors, or extended family member. And when there are no others around to share it with, you can deliver it out loud to yourself, as if you were delivering it to others. When we deliver what we have received to others, the knowledge we share deepens within ourselves. It works much like a testimony. The more you share it, the stronger and more firmly implanted the knowledge becomes. The more you deliver or share your Old Testament insights with others, the more deeply they will become imbedded into your own memory.

The Lord gives an interesting promise in Doctrine and Covenants 88:78 where he says, "Teach ye diligently and my grace shall attend you, that you may be instructed more perfectly in theory, in principle, in doctrine, in the law of the gospel, in all things that pertain unto the kingdom of God, that are expedient for you to understand."

Note the Lord says that when we teach diligently, by the grace of God, we are "instructed more perfectly." Teaching apparently facilitates the teacher's learning.

Most teachers will tell you that they learn much more in preparing and delivering their lessons than their students do. First because they have to pay closer attention, get more involved, relate it to other information, and make it clearer. Second, because in the process of delivery, the information is burned more deeply into their own brains. I remember learning this principle once in Primary when I had to give a short talk. I learned a lot more from that experience than when I just sat and heard other kids give their talks.

The Deliver Principle: The more we deliver or share what we have learned, the greater will be our ability to remember that information when needed.

The Deliver Habit: Deliver or share new information that you have learned with others, or at least deliver it to yourself, in a dramatic or memorable way.

The Seven Principles for Making a Memorable RECORD

In review, the A RECORD formula and principles are as follows.

- **A** is for *attention:* The more attention we pay to whatever we see or hear, the easier it will be to remember.

- **R** is for *relate:* The more we can relate new information to past, easily recalled information, the easier it will be to remember.

- **E** is for *envision:* The more vividly we can envision, or picture in our imagination, what we read or hear, the easier it will be to remember when needed.

- **C** is for *concrete:* Concrete, visible objects are pictured and remembered more easily than less tangible concepts or ideas.

- **O** is for *organize:* The more we organize information in ways that are meaningful to us, the easier it will be for us to remember.

- **R** is for *rehearse:* The more frequently and actively we rehearse information, the greater our ability to remember that information when needed.

- **D** is for *deliver:* The more we deliver or share what we have learned, the greater our ability to remember that information when needed.

How to Remember the A RECORD Formula

It will be important for you to cement this formula into your brain because these seven principles provide the foundation you will need for the procedures and techniques that follow. Moreover, if you experience difficulty in recalling information from your studies, these can provide a good checklist for troubleshooting. Finally, with an awareness of these principles you will be able to add your own memory techniques as needed.

Since an awareness of each point in this formula is so essential to understanding all that follows, let's take a few minutes right now to commit it to memory. Make sure this acronym and its related principles are firmly fixed in your long-term memory before you continue reading. To do this, let's apply some of the principles and methods we have just learned.

If you've read to this point, at least you've been giving this formula a significant amount of *attention*. Plus, you have *related* the acronym A RECORD with its associated principles. If you have also *envisioned* or pictured yourself doing these things, that should help to etch the principles into your brain, especially if your images were *concrete* enough.

By relating these principles to the acronym, you have an *organized* way to remember them. Plus, you will note that they are organized pretty much sequentially. In other words, whenever you go about remembering something, you typically go through the process in this order. In fact, this is the basic habit or sequence for learning that we need to *rehearse* over and over again. In other words, whenever we are learning something new, we must first pay close attention and then relate it so something familiar and, in the process, envision this relationship or association in some concrete, organized manner.

Finally, we must make time to rehearse what we have learned and deliver it to others in order to burn it more deeply into our brain. This is the seven-step process of learning and remembering, which we must apply and follow over and over until it becomes a habit. But once that habit is formed, you will find that your recall ability has skyrocketed! By now you should have this formula stored in your mind fairly well. But just to make sure, here is a little exercise I would like you to try:

On the left hand side of a blank sheet of paper, write the acronym vertically:

A

R

E

C

O

R

D

If you can't remember all seven letters, just think, "In order for me to remember what I read in the Old Testament, I must be like the prophets of old, and make A RECORD of the things I want to remember."

Once you have the letters A RECORD written vertically on your paper, write down—from memory—what each letter stands for. If you miss a principle, look it up, but then put the book down and write it from memory.

Next, turn the paper over, think of the acronym clue phrase, "In order for me to remember, I must be like the prophets of old and make A RECORD." Then write down the letters vertically again and note what each one stands for. This time, include as much information about the principle as you can recall. As you do this, Envision yourself doing each step with some information you are learning or would like to remember from the Old Testament.

When you are done with this you should have this acronym, along with these seven principles, chiseled into your brain. But to make sure the image doesn't fade, do this exercise once more after you are done with this chapter, and then again tomorrow, the next day, and at least once next week and each week thereafter for the next month. By then, this formula will be well in mind and ready to apply anytime, anyplace, and anywhere until it becomes a habit.

The Seven Habits of Effective Learners— in Review

- **The Attention Habit:** Pay close attention to, and get involved with, those things that you wish to remember.

- **The Relate Habit:** Relate new information in memorable ways (concrete, easily envisioned) with past familiar and easily recalled information.

- **The Envision Habit:** Envision or picture what you wish to remember with as much sensory-rich detail and as vividly as you can.

- **The Concrete Habit:** Picture concrete objects or symbols to represent less tangible concepts or ideas.

- **The Organizing Habit:** Organize what you wish to remember in ways that are meaningful to and memorable for you.

- **The Rehearsal Habit:** Actively rehearse what you have learned at regular intervals as needed.

- **The Deliver Habit:** Deliver or share new information that you have learned with others, or at least deliver it to yourself, in a dramatic or memorable way.

Notes

1. Stephen R. Covey, *The Seven Habits of Highly Effective People.*

2. Joseph Smith, *Millennial Star* 13 (15 November 1851): 339.

3. These are often referred to as *mnemonic* devices. The term mnemonic is derived from Mnemosyne, the Greek goddess of memory. The early Greeks invented some of these methods.

4. We could call this the *share* principle, but **S** does not fit our acronym. In addition, sharing implies a need for others, and you can actually "deliver" a

sermon to yourself with similar effect. But in your mind, you should associate *deliver* with sharing or teaching the information to others.

4

LEARNING WITH STYLE

In applying the principles cited in previous chapters, we must recognize that different people have different styles of learning. Certain methods will likely work better for some readers than for others. However, each style has its advantages.

There are two basic learning styles or preferences: visual and auditory or verbal. If I ask what you remember about Moses, or the book of Isaiah, what would you recall? If images of Moses' exodus or images from Isaiah—such as the "mountain of the Lord's house"—immediately came to mind, then you are likely a visual person. But if the words of Moses or the teachings of

Isaiah are what you first recalled, then perhaps your style is more auditory. The following quiz may help you discover which style or mode of learning works best for you.

Learning Style Quiz
(check the ones that apply)

I seem to remember better
_____ when I see things.
_____ when I hear things.

When listening to a lecture I sometimes like to
_____ doodle.
_____ focus on the nature of the words used.

When attending a class I would prefer the instructor
_____ provide good visual aids.
_____ explain in detail what she is talking about.

When reading, I can remember the material better if
_____ I visualize the events in my mind.
_____ I read out loud.

When learning about another country, I would rather
_____ see a movie showing different locations.
_____ have someone tell me about the place or hear music
from the country.

When I try to remember things, I do better when
_____ I visualize the setting where I learned the
material.
_____ I remember hearing the information.

I can memorize information better when
_____ I visualize the events or words on the page.
_____ I recite the information over and over.

As you've probably guessed, those who select the first option most often are more visually inclined. Those who select the second option more often do better with more auditory or verbal methods of learning. Most of the methods in the next four chapters are designed for the visual learner because the majority of us are better suited for that method of learning; in addition, many of us have good capacities in both areas. However, I have included adaptations and other tips for those who prefer a more auditory approach.

One student said, "All my life I've been using visual study methods such as highlighting and reading over my notes, never understanding why I got little benefit from all my study time. Now that I understand my auditory learning style, I'm investing more time into reciting, discussing, and making and listening to tapes. The information seems to 'stick' so much more easily. I feel smarter!"

Have you ever realized your concentration is much better in the morning than at night, or vice versa? Do you prefer working alone, with a partner, or in a group? Do you learn better when you are more involved, or relaxed? Do you like to make lists, or would you prefer a creative collage?

If you could establish the ideal study environment for yourself, what you would include? Would it be quiet, or would there be music? Would you prefer it light and bright? Or dim and cozy? Would you choose a beanbag or sturdy chair and table?

These all relate to other learning preferences you may have. The following quiz may help to clarify these as well.

Directions: Circle the answer that best describes you, or fill in the blanks to help identify your learning preferences.

I concentrate better in the
    morning.
    evening.
    _____.

I prefer studying
    alone.
    with a partner.
    in a group.
    (combination)

I learn better when I am more
    involved.
    relaxed.

I like to
    make lists.
    draw pictures.
    create a collage.

I prefer studying when
    it's quiet.
    I have soft music.
    I have music with a beat.
    _____.

When I read, I prefer
    a bright room.
    a dim and cozy environment.

When I study I prefer to
    sit at a table.
    relax in a bean bag.
    _____.

These are all elements of your unique learning style. We all have our own preferences and ideal learning style, including the instructional method; the environment and social grouping; and the time of day in which we generally learn most effectively. Knowing your learning style can make a significant difference in your ability to recall what you've read. Think about it. Look at the elements you circled and then design your ideal study environment. Next, identify the time that you study most effectively. These two simple things may make a dramatic difference in your ability to learn—and remember.

If I could create my ideal learning environment, it would be as follows:

QUIET, WELL LIT TABLE, CHAIR, GOOD ELBOW
ROOM, ROOM TO STRETCH & EXERCISE/ EVERY 45 MINS
to AN HOUR

Of course, we can't always have the ideal learning conditions, and we should be able to learn under most conditions. But the more we can learn about our specific preferences and style—and then create that environment or type of learning situation for ourselves—the more effective our study sessions will be and the more information we will retain.

5

THE AMAZING MEMORY METHODS—TEN OPTIMIZING STRATEGIES

If you have ever seen someone perform a truly amazing memory feat, you've seen the power of these principles in action and the potential of a trained memory. Typical examples might include remembering the name and birth date of everyone in an audience, after only brief introductions; remembering a twenty-plus digit number in perfect order; or being able to recite or describe the contents of every page in a magazine. How do these people accomplish these seemingly miraculous feats?

Most likely, such individuals are either savants or mne-monists[1]—or ordinary people like you and me who know and use the methods described in this chapter.

Savants, like the man depicted in the movie *Rain Man*, have a natural, better-than-photographic memory that enables them to effortlessly perform astounding feats of memory. Some scholars believe we all have that potential; it's simply shrouded in a veil of forgetfulness, and after we die and return to the other side, this ability will be restored.

Orson Pratt noted that "the spirit has not lost its capacity for memory, but it is the organization of the tabernacle that prevents it from remembering." However, he continued, when the spirit leaves the body and is no longer subject to its limitations and infirmities, "then is the time we shall have the most *vivid knowledge of all the past acts* of our lives during our probationary state." The spirit, Pratt added, "is a being that has capacity sufficient to retain all its past doings, whether they be good or bad. . . . And it is the reflection of the spirit memory that produces joy."[2]

Elder George Q. Cannon added that we will also remember everything we ever saw, not forgetting any scene. "Memory will be quickened to a wonderful extent. Every deed we have done will be brought to our recollection; every acquaintance made will be remembered. There will be no scenes or incidents in our lives that will be forgotten by us in the world to come."[3]

This quickening of the memory is reportedly a common experience after death, or even after a near-death experience, as reported in the annals of the International Association for Near-Death Studies (IANDS).[4] Hugh Nibley, the late BYU professor of ancient languages and texts who was well known for his extraordinary memory, may have experienced such a quickening of memory. Less well known is the fact that while in his early twenties he had a near-death experience in which he actually passed to the other side. Before this experience, he was apparently always interested in learning, receiving special tutoring as a child, but this event may have had an enhancing effect on his memory.[5]

That's something nice to think about—that someday we may all have that ability. The obvious catch, however, is that it appears one has to die to obtain it. Personally, for now at least, I am content with less lethal methods. Fortunately they are available, as many memory masters and performers have demonstrated.

These memory masters, or mnemonists, accomplish their feats by employing A RECORD principles, as well as by utilizing the following advanced strategies or techniques in applying those principles. Note that most of these strategies are based upon one or more of the principles we've already discussed, particularly the Envision and Relate Principles. In fact, these ideas are simply ways to make these processes and mental pictures more powerful.

Avoiding the Profane

Some memory methods pose a problem, at least for me. Most of the books and courses on memory-enhancement strategies suggest that for an association to be vivid or memorable, it needs to be in some way bizarre, exaggerated, distorted, farcical, zany, ludicrous, or outrageous—anything but ordinary; some even suggest the association have a sexual connotation or association.

While bizarre, farcical, and zany techniques may be okay when trying to recall jokes, when we are concentrating on concepts or teachings of salvation from the scriptures, including prophecies of Christ, these image qualities don't seem appropriate. Some might even be considered profane, vulgar, or sacrilegious.

On the other hand, the idea that unusual or extraordinary things are more easily remembered is undeniable. Likely one reason Joseph Smith was able to accurately recount what the angel Moroni taught him in his room, as recorded in the Pearl of Great Price, was because the visitation was so extraordinary, as well as the fact that it was repeated three times.

On this subject, Truman Madsen, former director of the Judeo-Christian Studies Center at Brigham Young University, noted that "many systems encourage you to make sensible, or logically appropriate symbols. Depending on the subject matter, either may be preferred. But generally, you are almost certain to remember an outlandish image more clearly than an ordinary one.[6]

Note that Brother Madsen says "depending on the subject matter." Although this quote was not in the context of remembering scriptures, the principle still applies: things that are unusual are often easier to remember.

Regarding imagery of a sexual nature, some scenes from the Old Testament, if depicted in a movie, would likely result in an R rating. After all, there is a lot of "begetting," "knowing," "lying with," and even more explicit language in the Old Testament. However, those scenes are not usually the most important to remember or to pass on to posterity. So I see no need for the use of intimate imagery here. In fact, it could be distracting.[7] (See chapter 11 for an example of how these methods and the seven habits can actually be used to overcome destructive habits, including addiction to pornography).

What you will find below are the clean-cut strategies for enhancing mental images. And, in fact, some research[8] suggests that these methods can be as effective when studying the scriptures as the more bizarre, profane, and potentially distracting strategies. This is especially true when facilitated by the Holy Spirit, which is able to "bring all things to your remembrance" (John 4:26; see also chapter 12 in this book).

Ten Methods for Creating Indelible Images

As noted in the E principle taught earlier, we are able to remember stories and ideas much better if we can *envision* (create a clear, vivid picture of) them in our mind. Here then are less bizarre—but no less effective—ways to make mental images and associations more memorable.

1. **Amplify** aspects of what you want to remember by making them larger, longer, taller, bigger, fatter, or in some other way more exaggerated than normal. To remember the book of Numbers, for example, I imagine numbers eight feet tall. You could change the shape or color of images in your picture. (You'll see how I use this

below to help distinguish text from memory cues).

2. **Create action** or motion in your images of the text. See things rising, falling, twisting, jerking, expanding, shrinking, and so on. The Old Testament uses many imagery and action verbs that lend themselves well to this approach. For example it's easy to imagine—and therefore remember—the stories of the walls of Jericho "tumbling down"; Jonah being swallowed by a giant (amplified) fish; or Samson "rending" the lion. It may also be helpful to take advantage of the action imagery to envision more conceptual teachings such as God "opening the windows of heaven and pouring out a blessing" to those who pay their tithing (Malachi 3:10).

3. **See interaction** between the elements of the message or text, ideally a specific setting. We can imagine Jacob wrestling with an angel at Peniel or Joseph's brothers throwing him into a pit. Again, the Old Testament provides lots of memorable inter-action if we just take a second to visualize it.

You can also use this method to bring concepts and prin-ciples to life. Let's take, for example, the concept that "to obey is better than sacrifice" (1 Samuel 15:22). Keep in mind that this is my own mental creation, or personal movie, of this scene and story. As the director of my own mental movie, I will take some literary license with the dialogue and props, making this scene more memorable for me while retaining the essence of the story.

So I imagine Samuel talking with King Saul near an altar. I imagine Samuel seeing and hearing bleating sheep and oxen behind Saul (v. 14). Then I imagine him asking (my paraphrase), "What are these doing here? Did not God command you to destroy all that they have?" (vv. 14, 3, 18). I then imagine Saul grabbing one of the rams by the horns and throwing him onto the altar (this action is a visual reminder that we are talking about sacrifice) with the whiny excuse, "But the people took of the spoil, sheep and oxen, the chief of the things that should have been utterly destroyed, to sacrifice unto the Lord" (v. 21).

Then I see and hear Samuel, somewhat perturbed, make that famous utterance: "Behold, to obey is better than sacrifice, and to hearken than the fat of rams" (v. 22). Creating this imagery can be fun, and most of the elements needed to do so are already in the text, or easily created. And such a picture vividly imagined will not soon be forgotten.

4. **Create unusual, outlandish, or unconventional** images or associations. If you saw a dog bite a man, it may get your attention, but it's not that extraordinary. However, if you saw a man bite a dog, that would likely be more memorable. (See the number pegs in chapter 6 for additional illustrations.)

5. **See yourself in the scenes**. Get involved. For example, I can envision myself with Gideon surrounded by Midianites. I can imagine myself lapping water with my hand, and so being selected as one of three hundred whom the Lord used to defeat the Midianites with trumpets, empty pitchers, and lamps (see Judges 7). I could also imagine myself as Joseph being thrown into the pit or sold into slavery (see Genesis 37); as Daniel in the den, running my fingers through a lion's mane (see Daniel 6); or as Jonah sitting in a whale's belly, lamenting my reluctance to warn Nineveh (see Jonah 2).

6. **Use symbols** or easily pictured objects to represent common concepts. For example, a chocolate heart to represent love, a shield to represent honor, a dove with an olive branch to represent peace, or scales to represent justice. As noted in chapter 1, the Israelites apparently did this. For example, they use a stiff neck to represent pride, a hard heart to represent stubborn unwillingness, and so on. (See 2 Chronicles 36:13.)

7. **Develop and use *your own*** creative images and symbols to make effective associations. Don't stick to mine or anyone else's. The more involved you become in developing these images and symbols, the more attention you will be paying to text and the more you will remember. And as with other methods mentioned here, creating your own symbols to represent various concepts can be fun. Our children enjoy developing creative, memorable symbols and associations as a travel game while riding in the car.

Just a tip: you will usually remember best the first concrete image that comes to your mind.

8. **Draw pictures and symbols** to represent the concepts you want to remember the most. You don't have to be a Leonardo da Vinci. Stick figures work fine; pen or pencil doodles equally effective. What matters is that you know what the images stand for. Pictures and symbols are especially helpful for visual learners, but they are also effective for those who are more right brained, those with greater tactile sensitivity, or other creative individuals (see chapter 7 for a well-developed system that makes good use of this technique).

9. **Involve other senses in your imagery**; add sound, touch, taste, and even smell to your pictures. Some people naturally experience these senses more than others, and recalling a certain feel, taste, or smell can evoke associated memories. Even if you are sensory-challenged to some degree, adding or imagining other senses in your mental pictures brings the Old Testament stories more to life, and makes your images more memorable. So you might imagine what Isaac felt and smelled when he felt Jacob dressed as Esau or the sound of God's voice on Sinai announcing to Moses, "I am that I am" (Exodus 3:14). Imagine the taste of manna in the desert (see Exodus 16:31 for a hint) or the "smell of myrrh and aloes" (Psalm 45:8). Sensory-rich experiences are more easily recalled than simple black-and-white silent pictures.

10. **Read aloud, hear, and discuss.** If you are more auditory or verbally oriented, enhance your images—or at least your recall of the text—by reading the words aloud or onto a cassette and then by listening as you drive in the car. Some research suggests your own voice may be more memorable than someone else's. You might also find it helpful to discuss with someone else what you're reading and how you might apply it to your life. This would likely work well for anyone, regardless of their learning preference. That's why we have Sunday School classes where teachers are counseled in the manual to involve class members "so all may be edified of all" (D&C 88:122).

One of the most important keys here is that whenever you employ one of these memory enhancement techniques, you have to first pay close attention and become involved with the text and message. Consequently, it can't help but become more memorable for you. (See how others get involved with the text, including yours truly, in chapters 7–9.)

Linking Concepts for Recall and Application

The ten strategies noted above are powerful and can indeed optimize your mental images and significantly improve your quality of memory storage and ease of retrieval. However, you'll only enjoy these results if you *use* these strategies.

If after reading these you say, "Oh, yeah, that makes sense. I could do that," but then you don't, what good will this do you? The answer? No good at all. So now you'll learn a way to remember these ideas for future application.

In chapter 11, I'll show you two methods for making the application of these techniques a habit. In chapter 6, you will learn a technique for recalling these techniques by their numbers. However, first I want to share another method for burning these ten optimizing strategies into your brain. Moreover, this technique can also be used to string together and remember any list of items, concepts, or ideas, including the order of the books of the Old Testament. Thus it is called the link method.

This method is an extension of strategy 3 noted above, plus the R and E Principles. It's simple to learn. In fact, it is often the first technique taught in memory enhancement courses. All you have to do is *envision a memorable interaction between items or key elements in your list.*

In order to make these interactions more memorable, it will be helpful to apply some of these ten techniques as you go. I will get you started by providing the key elements of each strategy and the interconnections I have envisioned for the first five so that you can see how this works. Then you can come up with images to link the last five.

- **Amplify the image** making it longer, taller, bigger, fatter, exaggerated.

- **Create action.**
- **See interaction** among the elements in your picture.
- **Create unusual, outlandish, or unconventional** images or associations.
- **See yourself in the scenes.**

First, I see myself going over to the TV and adjusting the volume to *amplify* the sound. As I'm doing this, the whole screen begins to *amplify,* or enlarge, until it reaches the ceiling—about eight feet tall and twelve feet wide.

On the TV screen, I see a documentary on the filming of *The Ten Commandments.* The Israelites stand poised on the banks of the Red Sea. I hear the director call *"Action."* Moses lifts his rod, the giant waves part, and all the people start running across the sea bottom to the other side. They are followed by the chariots of Pharaoh, but before those in pursuit can reach the Israelites, the elements (water) comes crashing down, *interacting* with the Pharaoh's unfortunate followers. Well, drowning them actually.

Cecil B. DeMille says, "Wow, that's great *interaction.*" He then sees a red speedboat traveling across the water and declares. "That's *unusual.* In fact, it's more than unconventional, it's outlandish! They didn't have those back then!"

I then decide to get into the picture, so I dive into the tube. Next thing I know, I'm sitting in the speedboat skimming over the water and waving to DeMille on the bank. I can now really *see myself in the picture.*

There you go. Now it's your turn. Look at the last five strategies and think of a concrete way to represent each; then link them together in some zany or unusual motion picture, applying some of these techniques to make the images vivid and memorable. You may choose to continue my story line or come up with one of your own. Have fun!

- **Use symbols** or easily pictured objects to represent common concepts.

- **Develop and use** *your own* creative images and symbols.

- **Draw pictures and symbols** to represent the concepts.

- **Involve other senses (sound, touch, taste, and smell) in your imagery.**

- **Read aloud, hear, and discuss.**

Remembering the Books of the Old Testament

As I noted, this technique can be used for lots of things. Remembering items you need to pick up at the grocery store, for example, can provide valuable practice. Stacking is one associated technique often used for a grocery list. You might see a loaf of bread, and on top of the bread, a two-foot-high carton of milk. Then, draped over the milk a lumpy sack of potatoes, on top of the potatoes a giant frozen chicken, on that a box of laundry detergent, and then a carton of eggs, some of which are broken. You can see egg yolks dripping over the edge of the detergent, onto the chicken and potatoes, and so on. The more we use our imagination to create vivid pictures and dynamic or odd interactions, the more creative we will become.

Now let's apply this linking method to remembering the books of the Old Testament, in order—information that can be useful when trying to look up passages. The Old Testament contains thirty-nine books, so this will take a bit more time than the grocery list, but I will get you started.

For this example, I'll use a different strategy. Most of the books in the Old Testament have the names of prophets or other significant people. For books such as Psalms and Proverbs, I imagine their writers.

Fortunately, I have friends with the same names as some of these Old Testament characters, so I can visualize my friends interacting with other elements. All I need to do is make memorable connections between titles or persons and move on. However, in creating these links, you will see how helpful it is to use a symbol, or picture, to represent names or abstract words. For example, when I think of Exodus, I envision a camel; for Leviticus, I picture a pair of Levis.

Remember, things that are concrete and easy to visualize are usually easiest to recall. Keep this in mind because whenever you're storing things in sequence, whether they are books of the Bible, long passages of scripture, or grocery items, the things in the middle are usually hardest to recall. So after your first few connections, be sure to use some of the ten optimizing strategies.

So, here are the first thirteen books of the Old Testament, with the symbols or persons I chose to represent them. Three of these books have basically the same name, which helps. Following the list are my visual linkages, or the connections I have pictured.

- Genesis: This is a no-brainer. I'm not going to forget this.

- Exodus: Camel with items strapped to its back.

- Leviticus: Levi jeans.

- Numbers: Giant numbers large enough to stand on.

- Deuteronomy: Moses and Aaron arm in arm singing a duet.

- Joshua: Joshua from *The Ten Commandments*, the movie.

- Judges: Two judges wearing their black robes.

- Ruth: A woman I know named Ruth.

- 1 Samuel: A guy I know named Sam.

- 2 Samuel: Sam again, this time looking much older with a beard.

- 1 Kings: A king wearing a crown.

- 2 Kings: Two kings joined at the back.

- 1 Chronicles: A newspaper—the *Daily Chronicle* rolled up.

- 2 Chronicles: Another newspaper, spread out.

Now to begin, I see a camel in a caravan (**Exodus**) with **Levi** jeans (Leviticus) on his hind legs, dragging a large **number 36** (number of chapters in Numbers, with the top part of the 6 hooked to the bottom of the number 3). Standing on the number 6 as it's being dragged along are Moses and Aaron, arm in arm, singing a duet (**Deuteronomy**). Aaron's left hand is stuck to **Joshua's** tar stick. Joshua (from the movie *Ten Commandments)* is holding onto the other end of the stick; in his left hand, he has ahold of the black robes of two **judges**. A woman I know named **Ruth** has ahold of the second judge's black robes, which she uses to wipe her brow. Holding on to her left hand is a man I know named **Sam** (1 Samuel). In his left hand, he has ahold of another, older man's beard. This man looks just like him only older and with a long white beard (2 Samuel). The old man is waving a crown in his left hand, which belongs to one of the **kings** in royal robes walking behind him (1 Kings). Stuck to the back of the first and walking backward is another king (2 Kings), who has one huge newspaper (the *Daily Chronicle*) under his arm and is reading another (1 and 2 Chronicles).

Now it's your turn. The following are the other twenty-six books in the Old Testament. I've included my symbols for reference for the first few, but I suggest you use your own; you will remember them better.

Admittedly, this is a major task. You may want to break it up into two or three parts. Learn one part today, the next tomorrow, and so on. Although I was able to come up with visual links for all thirty-nine books in about one hour, I had to practice them several nights and mornings in a row before I was comfortable that I had all of them stored in order.

It's a good idea to review your major memory tasks just before going to bed, or even while in bed before you go to sleep. The brain seems to be able to store them more easily that way. One reason, of course, is because you then do not have other information coming in and displacing what you have just learned.

- Ezra: Old guy sitting in an easy (EZ) chair.
- Nehemiah: He has a skirt on with a hem at his knee.
- Esther: I think of a woman I know named Esther.
- Job: Job I picture as an older, balding man.
- Psalms: I picture David playing a harp and singing.
- Proverbs: I picture King Solomon with a white owl on his shoulder.
- Ecclesiastes: Egg shells.
- The Song of Solomon: Solomon with a harp
- Isaiah: A British-looking chap with a pipe like Sherlock Holmes, who likes to say, "I say, old boy . . ."
- Jeremiah: I see a friend named Jerry.
- Lamentations: An old man with a burlap sack filled with ashes, crying.
- Ezekiel
- Daniel
- Hosea
- Joel
- Amos
- Obadiah
- Jonah
- Micah
- Nahum
- Habakkuk
- Zephaniah
- Haggai
- Zechariah
- Malachi

As noted above, after a couple of days I still had some difficulty recalling some of the connections. I couldn't see and place all of the titles at once, like I wanted to. So I decided to review and reinforce the organization of the books and logical associations. Of course, after Genesis the next three books have to do with the Exodus and traveling in the desert, and because they were at the beginning of the Bible, my associations worked well to keep them in order. Joshua of course took over after Moses, and after him it was the Judges. I didn't have a problem with Ruth.

There are only two books named after women. I initially imagined her wiping her brow on his robe, but seeing her plead for justice would also have been logical. I had some problems with Samuel. I couldn't always see who was holding on to Ruth's hand. But the Sam I envisioned had lost part of his index finger. So clarifying that hand clasp, seeing Ruth feel and remark about the partial finger helped me recall Sam.

Then I realized that ten of the next fourteen books had to do with the life and times of David. I knew the prophet Samuel was the one who called David. David of course became the next King. And then the Kings had their Chronicles, or writings. After Chronicles I make a good, vivid connection to Ezra sitting in an EZ chair, and remember that there are four books between Kings and the writings of David and Solomon, his son. One of those books was named after the other woman Esther, who was followed by poor old (later, rich old) Job. After Job we have the writings of David, Psalms, followed by the three books his wise son Solomon wrote. After the Song of Solomon we move into the stories of the other Old Testament prophets. But by then I had more than half of the books down. From this I think you can also see how a review of the text and the logical order of events, or the big picture, can help keep these extraordinary or mnemonic pictures and visual associations in order.

Now if you find that after lots of creative thinking you still need a few hints to help you with these links, either for the Ten Strategies, or the books of the Old Testament; you can check out what I came up with in the appendix.

However, for the sake of your memory, I encourage you *not* to peek at the appendix until you have done all that you can on this exercise first. Otherwise, if you just rely on my imagery, it will be like trying to free a butterfly from of its cocoon. If you don't do these exercises on your own, your memory will never develop the mental strength needed to fly into the realms of desired possibilities.

For additional examples and tips on creating vivid mental images and memorable links, check out postings under chapter 5 on my website at www.arecord4lds.com

Notes

1. Someone who actively practices mnemonics, or memory enhancement strategies and techniques (see chapter 3, note 2).

2. In *Journal of Discourses* 2:239, 240; emphasis added.

3. *Deseret Weekly* 38 (7 April 1889): 677; quoted in George Q. Cannon, *Gospel Truth: Discourses and Writings of George Q. Cannon.*

4. See www.iands.org and Raymond Moody's *Life after Life: The Investigation of a Phenomenon—Survival of Bodily Death* (New York: Bantam, 1975) for illustrations.

5. This experience was verified in a conversation with Phyllis Nibley, wife of Hugh Nibley, on December 2, 2005. For more information on the intellectually enhancing effects of NDEs, go to www.iands.org/aftereffects.html, or see Kenneth Rings, *Heading toward Omega* (Scranton, Penn.: William Morrow, 1984), 242–43.

6. Truman G. Madsen, *How to Stop Forgetting and Start Remembering, a Practical Digest*, 27. This is a great little book, but it's out of print. For a more recent book on this topic from a BYU professor, see Kenneth L. Higbee, *Your Memory: How It Works and How to Improve It* (New York: Avon Publishing, 1977). He reviews and advocates most of the methods shown in this chapter and in chapter 6.

7. Images of a sexual nature can cause an increased release of norepinephrine, which can imprint an image more indelibly into the brain. But this can also distract from less provocative memories and explains one reason that pornographic images can be so overpowering and hard to get out of one's head.

8. See Kenneth L. Higbee, *Your Memory: How It Works and How to Improve It.*

6

HOW TO REMEMBER WHO SAID WHAT AND WHERE THEY SAID IT

Let's say you have a sixteen-year-old son, who is assigned as a home teacher. One of the families he is assigned to visit has a son his same age. This young man has recently stopped attending church and has become involved with a gang. Your son doesn't see the value of visiting this family, however, and would rather hang with his close friends than try to fellowship their son. His excuse? "He has his agency. If he chooses not to go to church, that's his choice. If he ends up in prison, that's his problem. Just because I'm assigned to be his home teacher, I'm not responsible for his choices."

How, you wonder, can you help him to realize the importance of his responsibility? You recall that somewhere in the Old Testament there were pretty stiff consequences for those called to be watchmen who were negligent in their duties. But who said it? And where can you find it?

In this chapter, we explore how to create ironclad associations, so you will always be able to easily remember who said what, and where they said it.

Who Said That?

Most books on how to improve your memory have a section on how to remember names and faces, an important social skill. The same method can be applied here. When we're trying to remember what's been said in the Old Testament, we don't have to worry about faces. You can give Old Testament writers any face you choose. Because, of course, no one knows what they really looked like.

And remembering most of the relevant names shouldn't be so difficult either. Of course, we find a lot of new and somewhat difficult names in the Old Testament, but relatively few of those people wrote important historical information, provided recorded sermons, or said or did other things that are essential to remember.

Who cares if the prince of the eunuchs called Daniel, son of Judah, Belteshazzar? Or that the master of the eunuchs was named Ashpenaz? What's important is what Daniel and the other three sons of Judah did—their examples of faith and courage and where to find their story.

If it's not relevant to my salvation, or the salvation and progression of others, or even to understanding the events in the Bible, why bother learning it? I try not to waste my time with totally useless trivia. We only have so much time on this earth to prepare to meet God, so I don't usually use my time, or my limited brainpower, to remember trivia, even if it is in scripture. Perhaps someday I will need to know a trivial item, but when that day comes, I'll look it up and get it down. Until then there's more important stuff to remember.

Most names that are important to remember from the Old Testament are household names, names we've heard since our youth. You're not going to forget Adam or Eve; Cain or Abel; or Abraham, Isaac, and Jacob. And how could you possibly forget Noah, Joseph, Moses, Aaron, Solomon, or David? Add to that list Samuel, Ruth, Esther, Job, Isaiah, Jeremiah, Ezekiel, Daniel, Hosea, Joel, Amos, Jonah, and a few others, and you pretty much have listed the most important names to remember.

Admittedly, there are a few harder names, like Obadiah, Habakkuk, Zephaniah, and Nebuchadnezzar. And I'll show you how to remember those. But they didn't write or say a lot. And there are a few other important names, like Ishmael, Jonah, Saul, Gideon, Sampson, Elijah, and Elias, but not that many, especially if you narrow your focus to who said or did important things or made major contributions. Nevertheless, you will encounter a significant number of strange names you will want to remember. So here are the guidelines for remembering names and tying them to significant lessons, quotes, or events of their time.

1. **Make an association**. Find some part of the name that you can associate with a person, thing, or action that you are already familiar with. I'll use the name Nebuchadnezzar for an example, since that is not a common name, nor does it sounds like anything I'm familiar with. However, let's break it down. The *Ne* sounds like knee, *buch* sounds like book, and *nezzar* sounds like sneezer. So to remember this king's name, I could imagine him *knee*ling on one knee on a *book* and s*nee*zing—Ne buch ad nezzar. Remember your clue doesn't have to be identical to the name, or even sound identical to that which you need to remember. You simply need a reminder, a hint close enough to trigger your natural recall ability. In fact, since you've likely heard this name many times before, *knee-book*, or even *nab*, as in to seize or grab, would likely be enough to trigger a total recall of his name.

2. **Tie to text.** Tie the words or phrase used to remember

the name to a key phrase or idea you want to remember in the text. Take King Nebuchadnezzar's dream, for example, which no one could discern or interpret except Daniel. So I'll picture him kneeling on one knee on a book and sneezing on the iron- and clay-wrought feet of the image in his dream, as Daniel recounts it for him. You know the rest of the story—the stone cut out of the mountain without hands, etc., and could easily imagine it, as well as the implications for the rolling forth of the kingdom of God in the latter days.

3. **Write it.** Note the name, along with its more memorable picture association. Then, next to it or below it, note the quote, concept, or actions from the text that you want to remember. For instance:

Nebuchadnezzar:

- Though a king and a conqueror, he places his knee on a book and sneezes—thus kneel buch and [s]nezzar.

- Conquers Israel, dreams of an image in the latter days, befriends Daniel, who interprets his dream; is humbled to the depths of an animal but finally praises and gives glory to God.

4. **Periodic rehearsal**. Practice rehearsing the name and connection at spaced intervals. You may want to keep a list of these hard-to-remember names, along with their reminder picture, person, or phrase, and the related text or concepts you want to remember. Then periodically review your list.

One good way to do this would be to use the folded-paper technique noted in chapter 3. On the outside of the fold, write the concept or event you want to remember. Inside, write the name to be remembered. On the other inside fold, write the name reminder and link to the text. When you want to rehearse, all you have to do is pull out your paper. Fold it so all you can see are the concepts/events, and then try to recall the connection—who said or did that?

outside	inside left	inside right
Concept, lesson, or quote	Name	Clue
Dream about the latter-days	Nebuchadnezzar	Kneels on a book and sneezes

Again, as with most of the other memory-enhancement techniques, often all our memory needs is a bit of a hint, and it will take it from there and recall the rest of the story.

Let's illustrate these first three steps again, with three more names: Asenath, Absalom, and Rehoboam.

Association: Asenath—*Has in a bath.* Has her babies in a bathtub.

Text to remember: The daughter of Potipherah, wife of Joseph, mother of Ephraim and Manasseh.

Tied together: Asenath has her and Joseph's babies, Ephraim and Manasseh, in a fancy Egyptian bathtub while her father (wearing a flower pot on his head) and Joseph (wearing his multi-colored coat) look on.

Association: Absalom—*Abs* and *solemn.* He has a great set of abs (abdominal muscles), but he's very solemn.

Text to remember: Kills his brother for defiling his sister, flees the country, is finally reconciled with his father, David, but then turns against him and is killed, much to David's sorrow.

Tied together: I see Absalom with his shirt open, displaying an impressive set of abs, but he is solemn because he had his brother killed for defiling his sister. He then fled in exile. I see him return later and be reconciled with his father, David. But he turns on his father and is killed in battle, to David's sorrow.

Association: Rehoboam—*Re hoe boom.* I see him working on a plot of land in his garden, hoeing and hoeing, until it blows up in his face—boom!

Text to remember: The son of Solomon tries to reunite the Israelite kingdoms of the north and south, but they break up despite his efforts.

Tied together: I see him rehoeing two parcels of ground in his garden, first hoed and then given to him by his wise father, Solomon (represented by an owl sitting on a nearby perch). This garden is symbolic of the kingdoms in the north and south. He'd like them to grow together, but instead the whole garden blows up in his face and the kingdom becomes divided. I see the land splitting in two.

A note of caution: You will want to practice these names and connections periodically or they may fade into oblivion. One of my favorite mnemonic blunder stories is the tale of a young, rowdy college student introduced to a wealthy friend of the university named Mrs. Winbotam. (Now don't get ahead of me.)

He knew this might be an important name to remember, so utilizing his newly discovered mnemonic strategy for remembering names, he immediately imagined the woman sitting on a chair where wine had been spilled and getting her bottom soaked in wine, thus Mrs. Winbotam. Easy imagery. And he had no problem remembering her name the rest of the evening. But he was so impressed with himself that he never rehearsed.

Months later, he once again met the woman, and with supreme confidence he attempted to call her by name. Unfortunately, what came out of his mouth was not *Winbotam*. I'll leave the rest to your imagination. The moral of the story? It's important to write it down and do a few periodic reviews.

Where Is That Found?

Since our memories are never perfect, it's good to know where various teachings can be found in the Old Testament for easy reference. Even if you know a whole chapter verbatim, it's nice to know the chapter number, in case you quote something that your listener would later like to look up.

Several systems have been developed to help people remember numbers. These can easily be adapted for remembering page and chapter numbers, as well as the contents of these chapters or pages. I prefer to remember chapter numbers, since there are fewer of them than pages in the Old Testament, and because not all Bibles, especially electronic editions, have the same page numbering system. However, for the most part they share the same chapter divisions.

A Bit of History

The Numerical Order Alphabet, as it is called, goes back to at least 1648 when Stanislaus Mink von Wennsshein first introduced the concept. Dr. Richard Grey expanded on it in 1730. William James included it in his book *Principles of Psychology*, published in 1890. In 1886, in the fifth edition of *The World's Important Facts and How to Remember Them*, A. S. Boyd mentions that Professor Pliny Miles delivered lectures in 1856 that describe this system.

In this system, because numbers are abstractions that can be hard to remember, each number (0 through 9) was assigned a phonetic sound (as in Hebrew, these are all consonant sounds). Then easily imagined words made from these sounds were assigned to each number. The original system consisted of one hundred picture words representing the numbers one through one hundred.

Most modern memory performers or mnemonists use this or a similar system. We will use a similar system here. Many of the picture words have been changed or adapted to make them more concrete, memorable, or easier to link to the Old Testament, but the underlying phonetic numbering system has remained the same.

What follows are the numbers 1 through 10 with their corresponding phonetic sound. Be sure to read these as sounds rather than as letters.

1	t, d, th	t has only one downstroke
2	n	n has two downstrokes
3	m	m has three downstrokes
4	r	the fourth letter (sound) in four is an r
5	l	the Roman numeral 50 is L
6	j, sh, ch, soft g	reversed script j resembles 6
7	k, q, hard c, hard g	k looks like it has a reversed 7
8	f, v	script f resembles an 8
9	p, b	p is the mirror image of 9
0	z, s, soft c	z is for zero

For 6, the sound is a soft *sh* as in shoe, or *j* as in judge, or *ch* as in church. You could also use *g* as in gym. For 7, the sound is a hard *k* as in key, or *g* as in gate, or *c* as in cash. (Note this *c* has more of a *k* sound and is a much different sound than the *ch* in church.) By saying each sound associated with each number, you will soon be able to link the numbers with their associated sounds. The system is simple and ingenious.

If you run through the list a few times, you should find these easy to remember. But, at the end of this chapter, I've included another easy method for remembering this phonetic numbering system with associated "peg" words. (You don't even need to remember these sounds as long as you remember the picture words that go with each number.)

Once these basic sounds are firmly associated in your brain with their corresponding number, it's relatively easy to come up with words to represent larger numbers, especially two-digit numbers. For example, to represent the number twelve, you could use the words TiN, TeeN, ToNe, TuNe, TaN, DaN, DoNe, DuNe, DiNe, or DeN. For my purposes I usually use the word TiN, and I picture a TiN can. I selected a tin can because it is a concrete, familiar object that can easily be put into motion and linked to other objects with a little action—a swift kick. Can you see how these principles can work together with this system to create memorable images, linking chapter numbers to text content?

For example the first chapter 12 in the Old Testament is Genesis 12. This chapter contains the promise from the Lord to Abraham that in him "shall all families of the earth be blessed." After receiving this promise, Abraham departed with his wife and Lot and went down into Canaan, where he built an altar and called upon the Lord. Then when a famine arose, the family continued on into Egypt.

To link this story with the number twelve, I see Abraham handing out red tin cans to representatives from all the families of the earth. On the can it says, "Blessings from Abraham." I then see Abraham kick a can down the road to Canaan, where he builds an altar. I see the red can on the altar. Then Abraham takes the can off the altar and kicks it again toward Egypt. Once in Egypt, I see the can being kicked into the court of Pharaoh, where the Pharaoh demands, "What is this?"

The rest of the scenes and events in chapter 12 can be linked together from there, using the methods you learned in chapter 5 and the methods you will learn in chapters 7 and 9. So when you think of any event from chapter 12, it can lead you back to the memory peg word for that chapter, which in this case is TiN can.

Note the picture words used for numbers are often referred to as peg words or memory pegs because like pegs on a wall or hat stand, you can hang or attach other new or less memorable images to them. So of necessity these must be easily remembered words that are concrete or represent objects that are easy to picture.

Using the System to Teach a Lesson

Now, let's go back to our example at the beginning of this chapter. How could a father use this system to help his son better understand his responsibilities as a home teacher? Remember, the son had said, "Just 'cause I'm assigned to be his home teacher, I'm not responsible for his choices."

This statement reminded the father of a passage he'd read in the Old Testament. However, he could not remember where in the Old Testament the verse was located. Let's fix that. With a bit of effort and a good search tool, the father would find what he was looking for in Ezekiel 3, where we read, "Son of man, I have made thee a watchman unto the house of Israel: therefore hear the word at my mouth, and give them warning from me. . . . When a righteous man doth turn from his righteousness, and commit iniquity, and I lay a stumbling block before him, he shall die: because thou hast not given him warning, he shall die in his sin, and his righteousness which he hath done shall not be remembered; but his blood will I require at thine hand" (Ezekiel 3:17, 20).

Since the son is a teenager, it would likely be better for him to read this warning from the Lord right out of the scriptures rather than hearing it from his father.

So if this father were familiar with this peg system, here's what he might do so that next time he needs this scripture, he will be able to turn right to it.

First, he would need a word picture or phrase to remind him of Ezekiel. Personally I think of Ezek the Geek. And I imagine a patriarch with thick, dark-rimmed geeky glasses with taped corners and pens clipped to his robe.

Second, he would need to identify the peg word for the chapter number. An easily remembered peg word or symbol for the number three, which contains the *m* sound, is *mow,* an action that is easily visualized.

Third, he would create a picture linking Ezekiel and *mow* with key elements he wanted to remember from the text such

68

as a watchman on a tower who does not warn the people of an approaching enemy. People die as a result, and the watchman is held accountable. To tie these ideas together, the father could imagine a watchman on a tower sleeping, or playing cards with friends. Consequently, he does not see an enemy sneak in and begin to kill the citizens. Finally he hears the cries and runs to see what has happened. Ezekiel, who is wearing those geeky glasses and pushing a red lawn mower, meets him and declares, "For your negligence in not warning the people, their blood will I require at thy hand."

A few reviews of this scene, Ezek the geek with a red lawn *mow*er holding the watchman, who looks a lot like this son, responsible for not warning the people, and the concept and location will be firmly fixed in this father's memory, ready for the next teaching opportunity.

Cautions and Tips

There is a danger in using a peg system or introducing artificial elements into an Old Testament story to facilitate recall. If you are not careful, it may become difficult to distinguish between the organic elements of the text and the foreign aids to memory. Therefore, when developing my pegs and pictures, I've learned to do several things in order to help me keep these basic elements separate in my mind.

1. You will note that almost none of my peg words or images are used elsewhere in the Old Testament; there are no tins cans or lawn mowers in the text. And none of these objects, symbols, or actions would be common to normal Israelite activities. In fact, most of them, like Tie–1, TiN–12, or TiRe–14, are objects that were not invented until after the Old Testament was written. So if I see one of those in a scene I've created in my mind, I know that this represents the chapter number.

2. When I visualize these number pegs or symbols, I imagine them painted red. Thus they are truly extraordinary and, as noted

above, more memorable. But I know that red items in my pictures represent numbers, not text.

3. I am careful not to make these features more prominent in my mental movie than the actual text or message elements.

These three steps, used together, help prevent confusion between artificial memory devices and the message or concepts found in the book.

You'll see that most numbers could have several word options. However, it's usually best to use a standard list like the one provided below, so each number is always represented by the same word picture. On occasion, you may want to use two different words, or two separate word lists to represent the same numbers, for variety and adaptation. Or maybe you'll come up with picture peg words that work better for you. Great! Just keep one thing in mind: the peg words should either be associated, as with *oar* and *row*, or not used together in the same book or project. Otherwise, it could become confusing and less memorable. And that brings us to a final question.

Why I Don't Peg Verses

If this system works so well, why don't we use it to identify verse numbers as well? Besides the fact that it would take quite a bit of time and effort, it could become extremely confusing. While it is possible to develop two separate peg lists (I actually share two lists in this chapter), tying picture words from two lists into one text would be too distracting for most of us. In fact, it might even distort the message of the scriptures.

Identifying the chapter is usually good enough because most of us have either marked the verses in the chapter so we'll be able to find them, or we can see in our mind's eye the location of concepts within a chapter. Plus, as you will see in this chapter, if you commit to memory a chapter at a time, the most important concepts will be linked together in sequential order. So at least you will know if the concept or verse you are looking for comes at the first or last of the chapter. Then too, you can always look at the chapter summaries at the beginning of each chapter for a clue.

So let's review the entire primary number peg list. This list contains picture words that are familiar, concrete, easily imagined, conducive to action images, and in most cases modern or unusual for an Old Testament setting so as not to be easily confused with other things organic to the Old Testament.

Number Pegs for Remembering Chapters in the Old Testament

1. Tie	29. Nap (in a hammock)
2. Snow	30. Moss, moose
3. Mow (lawn mower)	31. Mitt (baseball mitt)
4. Row, oar	32. Man (man in black)
5. Law (a sheriff)	33. Mom (my mom)
6. Shoe	34. Hammer, mirror
7. Key	35. Mail (mailman or letters)
8. Sofa	36. Match (that you strike)
9. Pie	37. Mike (as in microphone)
10. Toes	38. Movie
11. Toad	39. Mop
12. Tin (can or cup)	40. Rose
13. Tomb (open grave or tombstone)	41. Radio
	42. Horn (bugle)
14. Tire	43. Ram (a Dodge Ram truck)
15. Towel	44. Rear (horse rearing up)
16. Dish	45. Root
17. Tack	46. Reel (fishing rod reeling something in)
18. TV, dove	
19. Tub	47. Rash (that itches)
20. Noose, newspaper	48. Rake
21. Net	49. Roof
22. Nun	50. Rope
23. Name (nameplate)	51. Lasso, or lace
24. Nero (fiddling)	52. Light (flashlight)
25. Nail	53. Lion
26. Nudge	54. Llama
27. Knock	55. Lure (fishing hook)
28. Knife	56. Lollypop

57. Leech	80. Fuse
58. Loaf (of bread)	81. Photo (snapping a photo)
59. Lap (laptop computer)	82. Fan
60. Jazz (saxophone)	83. Foam
61. Shot (with a needle)	84. Fur
62. Shin (kick in the)	85. Foil (tin foil)
63. Jam	86. Fish, effigy (hanging from
64. Chair	a rope)
65. Jell-O	87. Fig, fog
66. Judge (gavel)	88. Five
67. Shock	89. VIP
68. Shave (with a razor)	90. Pizza
69. Jeep	91. Bat
70. Gauze (bandage)	92. Piano
71. Kite	93. Bomb
72. Cane	94. Bury (cover with dirt)
73. Comb	95. Bell
74. Crow	96. Pitch (pitch a softball)
75. Coal	97. Pack (backpack)
76. Cage	98. Pave (paving a road with
77. Gag	asphalt)
78. Coffee	99. Pipe
79. Cape	100. Daises

(Note: Feel free to create your own list at any point, if you can come up with other words with the requisite consonant sounds, that are easier for you to remember. For another excellent list of associated words, see page 220 in *Your Memory: How It Works and How to Improve It*, by Kenneth Higbee. This is perhaps the best book available for further in-depth and authoritative yet easy reading on mnemonics.)

Practice going over these words on a regular basis to keep them fresh in your memory, at least until you've used them a number of times. After that, they will be easy to remember. But if you ever forget, simply sound out the sounds representing the number you want to recall and the peg word will be there waiting for you.

Remembering the Phonetic System and the Peg Words

In this section, I will share two different ways to remember this phonetic numbering system. First, to simply remember the sounds associated with each number, think of the following parts of your body, in order, from bottom to top.

> Sole (of your feet) gives the s sound for 0
> Toes give the t sound for 1
> Knee gives the n sound for 2
> Muscle gives the m sound for 3
> Rear end gives the r sound for 4
> Love handles give the l sound for 5
> Chest and shoulder give the ch and sh sounds for
> 6
> Collarbone gives the k sound for 7
> Face gives the f sound for 8
> Pate (top of head) gives the p sound for 9

Now go through this list and touch each body part as you say the associated sound. Do this three times today and three times tomorrow, and you'll soon have these sounds down. But these are not as important to learn as the first ten picture words. If you can remember these, they will also remind you of the ten phonetic sounds. Here is an easy way to remember those:

The letter t in tie looks like the number 1. Then the next three words rhyme—*snow, mow,* and *row. Law* is one vowel sound from *low,* which would rhyme with *row,* and a lawman's badge has five points. A shoe hanger looks like a 6. The number 7 is a key number in the Old Testament. The script *f*—the main consonant sound in *sofa*—looks like the number 8. The *p* in *pie* is a 9 in reverse. And the word *toes* for ten is easy. Just remember you have ten of them.

And if that doesn't help you remember, try linking them together like this. See yourself coming out of your house fixing your **tie**, and it's **snow**ing, but you can still see your neighbor mowing his lawn, and someone **row**ing by in a rowboat. A **law** man stops the boat and tells the passengers there is no rowing on pavement. "That is what a **shoe** is for," the lawman explains, "to walk on pavement." You decide this whole scene is too crazy for you, and you want to go back inside, but now you've locked the door. So you fumble for your **key**. Once inside, you flop down on the **sofa** and begin to eat your favorite **pie** as you play with your **toes**. Can you see that? You may be able to make up an even better story to remember these words. Try it!

Alternative Number Memory Systems

Since the need to recall the location of important text is as old as books, it's no wonder several systems have been developed to help people remember numbers in general, and page or chapter numbers in particular. There are also several ways to mentally tie this information effectively to the contents or concepts on those pages.

Another system I like is the rhyming system. This system has paired words that rhyme with each number. One popular form is as follows:

1. one—gun
2. two—shoe
3. three—tree
4. four—door
5. five—hive (bee)
6. six—sticks
7. seven—heaven
8. eight—gate
9. nine—dine
10. ten—hen

It's nice to have this second system as well, to help remember numbered items within a text, especially when the items number ten or fewer. You can, of course, use this system to remember higher numbers as well. In that case, you simply add the symbols. For example, for the number twenty-four, you would picture a shoe and a door. Of course, the phonetic numbering system is simpler for larger numbers (you only have to pair one object instead of two), which is why I use it as my primary system to remember chapters.

An obvious use for this rhyming system might be to help you remember the Ten Commandments in order, as well as the number that goes with each commandment.

Now that you understand the peg system and how it works, as well as how to make strong, unique, memorable associations, let's practice with the Ten Commandments. I've provided the peg symbols and each commandment (leaving off the "Thou shalts") in order. All you need to do is make up a memorable picture to tie them together and write that out to the side, in the space below each, or on a separate sheet of paper. (You'll need to come up with your own images and symbols to represent the pegs. I have noted my symbols and associations in the appendix, but don't look there until you've tried this yourself. Be creative and have fun!)

1. Gun—no other gods before me

2. Shoe—don't make unto thee any graven image

3. Tree—don't take the name of the Lord thy God in vain

4. Door—remember the Sabbath day, to keep it holy

5. Hive—honor thy father and thy mother

6. Sticks—don't kill

7. Heaven—don't commit adultery

8. Gate—don't steal

9. Dine—don't bear false witness against thy neighbor

10. Hen—don't covet

While you are at it, why don't you make an association to tie these to the chapter in Exodus where they can be found?

Of course, these answers are found in Exodus 20. The symbol I use to remind me of Exodus is a camel. You may recall from the phonetic peg list above one word for twenty is *noose*. So what sort of picture can you come up with to connect a camel, a noose, and a symbol for the Ten Commandments?

Go to my website at www.arecord4lds.com for examples of ways to remember the most important names of the Old Testament as well as how to remember the location of more than sixty of the greatest stories and teachings of the Old Testament, using this peg numbering system. Or you can simply have fun creating your own peg associations and memorable links.

7

MAPPING YOUR MEMORIES

Where there is no vision, the people perish.
—Proverbs 29:18

As noted in the Concrete Principle, most of us remember things we see much better than things we hear. Writing things out also helps to deepen the impression and preserve our memories. The following methods for storing memories, including memory mapping, is based on these two principles. These methods are also an extension of the Organization Principle. But how your brain organizes information, as you will soon see, may be quite different from most formal organization procedures or how an author has organized his information. It may be helpful to keep in mind that to *organize* may include the processes of summarizing, outlining, and classifying.

Of course, the Old Testament is organized into various books, basically in chronological order. It's further broken down into chapters and verses. All of this structure, framework, and background can assist in our recall of the information contained therein, as well as in finding or recalling the location of that information.

On Location

As I try to picture the events of the Old Testament, it helps to organize the events according to locations, where I imagine them taking place. This is especially helpful for those of us with strong *loci* memory (*loci* being the Greek word for place)—we associate memories with places. The ancient Greeks used a loci system to help them remember speeches. When giving a speech, they would imagine different concepts displayed in different rooms of a familiar location, like their house. Then, when giving their speech, in their mind they would go from room to room, recalling the content discussed or displayed in each room.

I've found that if I have a setting or set location in my mind for different events in the Bible, I can remember those events better by going to that location in my mind. So I have an image in my mind of the plains of Mamre, Egypt, the Red Sea, the wilderness, the land of Israel's inheritance, "a land of brooks of water, of fountains and depths that spring out of valleys and hills" (Deuteronomy 8:7), the valley (Jezreel) where Gideon defeated the Midianites, as well as the courts of David, Nebuchadnezzar, Solomon, and so forth. Then I imagine events being acted out in these settings. Whenever I want to recall an event, I just recall the setting, and the events usually appear in my mind as well.

There is another way in which loci memory works. If I think of something while driving home from work but later forget it, if

I go back in my mind to the location I was at when I was thinking about that idea, it helps me recall it. This same principle has been applied to study techniques. By recalling the classroom they were in when they learned something, most people are able to better recall what they learned there. Visualizing the test room when you're rehearsing for a test may also help you remember the material once you get into that setting.

If you have a strong loci memory, you may want to imagine the events of the Bible happening in places you are familiar with. I don't usually use this method. I prefer to imagine events in what I imagine to be their native setting. But I have used it on occasion with good success, particularly imagining the story of David, when he and I were both young boys tending animals. I could imagine David in the same field I was in, with his sling defending against the lion and the bear.

You may want to try imagining Old Testament events taking place in your neighborhood or home town. For example, you could imagine the events of Egypt taking place on the playground of your elementary school. And when they leave Egypt, you could imagine them trekking through the canal to the local park and then wandering in the park or outside your city limits for forty years. You could imagine the different events and teachings of Exodus, Deuteronomy, and Numbers taking place at different spots within that locale. For example, you might imagine the ordination of Aaron or the Lord appearing to Moses and the seventy elders of Israel occurring in front of the local park bower, which in your mental picture has been draped in material to look a lot like a tabernacle in the desert.

You could imagine your neighborhood to be the land of Israel's inheritance, and the various events from Samuel to Malachi occurring in your own backyard and those of your neighbors, as well as in other areas of the city that you are familiar with.

Of course, the downside of this approach is that these are very unrealistic and artificial settings. It's taking the Old Testament events out of context. But when we see any biblical or other scripture-based play or pageant, whether it's at the Hill Cumorah in New York; the hillside in Manti, Utah; in the theater at the local university or stake center; or even in a movie on Temple Square, these are all artificial settings.

Who knows what the actual setting was like when these events occurred? Even if we were to travel there now, the locations wouldn't look like they did three thousand years ago. So, it boils down to whatever works for you. If you can vividly imagine these events happening on the plains of Syria, or the valleys of Jordan, wonderful! But if you find it easier to picture more familiar places in your neighborhood or elsewhere, that may be helpful as well.

Organization in Books

All books are organized in a logical manner, and as noted, an awareness of this organization can help us to categorize and structure the information in such a way as to make it easier to remember. However, while our brains prefer organization and categories, and we need that for effective communication, they do not necessarily operate in this linear, sequential manner. Our brains are able to make numerous associations in various directions instantly, almost simultaneously. Our brains do not necessarily follow a linear path or make associations in only one direction. The challenge is creating memorable order out of these numerous and potentially chaotic possibilities.

As noted, there is a linear path and order provided in the Old Testament. However, this may not always be the easiest order for us to remember information in, or the easiest format. Here's another option you may want to consider:

Mapping for Memory

Since our brains do not usually operate sequentially, other means of organizing material have been developed and popularized in recent years that seem to be more in line with our natural mental processes. In the 1970s, memory expert Tony Buzan developed a technique for note taking that he believed was more in line with the way our brains actually work. He called this method mind mapping; I call it memory mapping. Whatever you call it, it's basically developing a map or small diagram to help you find or recapture a memory. The advantage of this technique is that it not only helps us organize information in a manner that seems more natural and logical, but it also requires a person to lay out a graphic diagram that, especially for the visual and visceral person, results in the information becoming more deeply imbedded in the memory and thus easier to recall than simple text on a page.

Generally, when we communicate, words are converted into pictures then back into words. Therefore, when we start with graphic images, we save a step, replacing the words with something easier for our brains to remember.

Memory mapping works well for preparing a plan of action, working through ideas alone or in a group, and delivering a speech. It also works well for taking notes during speeches and presentation, as well as for outlining articles and books.

The essence of memory mapping is selecting key concepts to remember as you read, and then organizing key words or symbols for these key concepts on paper in a way that seems logical and memorable. Generally, notes should be brief, consisting of perhaps three to five key words, or perhaps a representative picture or icon. The central idea is placed in a circle or box, usually near the center of the page on a blank sheet of paper. A number of other notes representing major subdivisions or associated ideas are then placed on the page and linked to the main concept or concepts by lines. These are called tree diagrams because they look somewhat like a tree, with the main concept in the middle and supporting concepts branching off from there.

The old Chinese proverb, "A picture is worth a thousand words," is absolutely true. When remembering a speech, only two to three words, or even a small picture or symbol with lines connecting supporting ideas in the address, will enable your mind to

recall the essence of those thousands of words in a logical, under-
standable manner.

The following simple sketch illustrates this point. Can you
guess the story this drawing represents? (See 1 Kings 3:16–28.)

In the same way, when you later review your memory-map
notes, a simple sketch from your notes or a circled word can bring
back the whole verse or section for instant recall.

Mapping Steps

One method often suggested for enhancing comprehension
and recall of read information is SQ4R: survey, question, read,
w(r)ite, recite, and review. This method deserves its own section,

but I have noted it here as a suggestion to help prepare you for the even more effective memory enhancement technique of memory mapping.

Studies that led to the development of SQ4R showed that students were able to retain more of their reading if they first did a quick *S*urvey of the material to get the main idea and then formulated a few *Q*uestions to ask themselves as they read it through. Then, of course, they would *R*ead it to find the answers to their questions; w*R*ite down their answers; practice *R*eciting the answers; and then at the end *R*eview what they had learned.

Now you may not always have time to use this approach. Indeed it wouldn't seem practical for casual reading. But when you find a chapter that is particularly insightful or full of wisdom that you want to remember, you may want to use SQ4R and then create a memory map and perhaps even a few other associations to secure it firmly and vividly into your memory for easy recall.

Below are the fundamental steps used in developing a memory map as they might apply to mapping a segment of the Old Testament.

1. Lay out a sheet of paper lengthwise, in landscape fashion. This gives you more room to work because images of stories run horizontally rather than vertically.

2. Review the chapter or verses to be mapped using SQ4R or at least by noting the main theme and supporting ideas. The summary before each chapter in the Old Testament will usually contain key words and concepts that you can build on. If I'm not sure what the main idea is, I like to jot down the possibilities on a separate sheet or along the left edge of my paper.

3. Note the main theme or concept near the center of your sheet that you want to remember. (I like to do my initial layout in pencil in case I want to change it; later I use colored pens or pencils.) Now record everything on paper according to the way you see the topic and supporting parts, not in a chronological order or necessarily in the order they are presented in the chapter. We have been conditioned to see the first lines of anything as the most important, but that's not necessarily so. In fact, in typical

chiasmic format, in which parts of the Old Testament are written, the main idea is in the middle.

4. When mapping for memory, you are in control of where to
put the most important—and least important—ideas. I generally
jot down the first related idea or theme to the left and midpage as
a start. The more important ideas are usually closer to the center,
with other ideas or quotes farther out or at the bottom. As you
discover other key points in the chapter, they can be placed in the
upper left corner of the page or on a separate sheet, in order as
they are presented in the text. This way, you use both sides of your
brain—the orderly left side and the more creative right side.

5. When mapping chapters in the Old Testament, I usually
note the concepts related to righteousness, or the requisites for
salvation, in the upper half of the sheet, with guidance from God,
or Jehovah, at the top. Any references to Satan, the pathways to
hell, destruction, and so on tend to be in the lower half of the
page. The key is to map out in a way that seems logical and most
memorable for you. And remember, usually the first scene or map
that comes to mind is what will work best for you.

6. The central theme can be enclosed in a geometric figure
such as a triangle, square, rectangle, hexagon, or pentagon. You
may want to use the number of major subdivisions of the theme to
help determine the shape of the box. Each major subdivision can
be attached to one of the points or planes of the box. For example,
a triangle would be used for a theme that has three major subdivisions. You can also use boxes or cloud shapes to enclose the ideas
represented by each of the major subdivisions. Or simply note
them above or below adjacent lines (see maps below).

7. Doodle simple line drawings, symbols, or icons wherever
possible to represent key words, objects, or concepts—whenever
you can, not just when mapping. These can be a great aid to your
memory. In time, you may even develop your own memory symbols or shorthand. As noted above, a symbol or small sketch is
often better than many words.

In the following example, I have included a few symbols that
I use to represent sheep, shepherd, hear, wisdom, broken heart,

men, Satan, the jaws of hell, justice, prayers to God (star pointing up), revelation (star pointing down), love, God watching over, and His awareness. Can you guess which is which? Try creating some of your own. This is actually how some writing systems were formed.

This diagram represents only a few of the many styles and

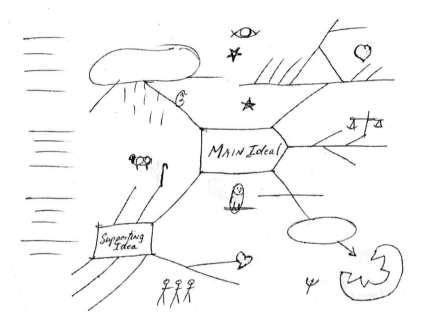

drawings you might use to structure what you read. Of course, key words would go within the shapes, or on the fishbone-like lines branching out.

8. As you read, note a word or symbol for each key idea. Try not to write more than three or four words per thought or verse. The fewer words, the better. Words are usually best printed rather than written in cursive. By keeping words to a minimum, you give those few words more power.

9. The basic structure of the map is open-ended. It proceeds from a center point outward. If one of these ideas becomes more involved, you may want to add additional major and supporting points on separate sheets.

10. A multicolored pen or pencil set can also help these

different ideas stand out. Assign black, blue, green, and red according to whatever scheme you design or how you *feel* about what you are making a note of. I suggest, however, that you keep your colors uniform. I use green for good and growth, blue for heavenly thoughts, and red for concepts related to unrighteousness, evil, dangers, or Satan. The more you are stimulated by color, shape, and light, the more you will want to involve and enrich your memories with color and feeling. Ideally, all images, including boxes, should have a color. (You may even want to color them with a pastel water color.) I use black or pencil to make connections, as well as lines, between ideas as I take notes. This becomes the thread that brings concepts together and lateral thinking into play, and it creates order or organization for later recall.

The following diagram contains a map I developed to help me remember God's response to Job in Job 38–42.

This may not be the neatest or most legible representation,

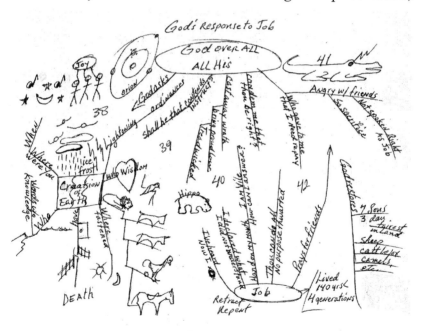

and the drawings certainly aren't the best. But it works to help me remember these important concepts. Note that there are actually several chapters represented here (I seldom do more than one at a time) with at least four pages of type, and nearly three thousand words summarized on this one page.

Don't worry about how messy and unorganized it looks. Neither the bishop nor your home teachers will be grading your paper; this is just for you. One reason memory mapping has had a tough time catching on in the school system is that teachers don't know how to grade such papers. But if this is helpful for you, that's all that matters.

Review your pictures at the end of your day, the following day, and one week later—then again every six months for continued retention to keep the pictures tied to the text. Once you recall something two or three times using memory mapping, especially if you can recreate it from memory, you will have locked in a memory pathway that can last a lifetime.

Notes and Observations

Doodling is primarily an activity of the right hemisphere of the brain, the artistic or creative side of us. As we begin to doodle, our brain shifts from high-frequency brainwave activity to a lower frequency. Thus you are shifting to an altered state of consciousness, which may facilitate encoding and memory. By working lists and sketches, you invoke both hemispheres, and the benefits can be enormous.

As a nice review, I sometimes like to diagram my most important chapters (such as Proverbs), observations, and so on on Powerpoint, using their various mapping tools. The following diagram shows the elements of a metaphor found in Hosea.

Symbol	Meaning
Eternal marriage (ch. 1)	Covenant relationship between God and Israel
Faithful husband	The Lord

Unfaithful wife	Children of Israel
Adultery	Departing from the Lord and ways of righteousness
Lovers	Other gods
Father (ch. 11)	The Lord
Son of Ephraim	The children of Israel
Divided heart	Trying to worship many gods
Sowing	Deeds, actions
Reaping	Reward or punishment for actions

This takes more time, but it is neater, cleaner, and easier to review, and I can usually get more on a page. More importantly, however, is that it again forces me to carefully review and become involved with the text and concepts, making me rethink their relationships. This process also requires the involvement of more of my brain; thus a deeper, broader, more lasting visual memory is formed.

Other people might have a difficult time understanding your notes or using them effectively, unless they participated in their creation. That's one reason I don't want you using mine. It will work far better if you can create your own, especially if you are a visual person. Then, when you glance at even a single page of your mapped notes, you will have near instant recall, and be able to deliver a fairly accurate playback of the concepts you heard, thought, or read, way back when you made those notes.

The trick is to convert what you read into images much like you might script a movie. Then use mapping to give those images some structure, listing the main idea, supporting ideas, and so on, and sketching out a few of those images, or symbols, to represent them, as well as the flow of ideas. Connect the concepts. Add details as necessary as if you were a movie scriptwriter or director imagining the scenes. Then connect it to the location of the actual text using the peg system so you will be able to easily recall where it is if you want to reference exactly what it says.

Unfortunately, most people do not utilize these organizing or note-taking methodologies often. But from now on, if you will make a conscious effort to organize or reorganize the information you read in the Old Testament in a way that's graphic and meaningful to you, I promise you will find yourself remembering it much better.

For more information on, and examples of, memory maps, go to www.arecord4lds.com

8

HOW TO MEMORIZE
LENGTHY PASSAGES

For most people, rote memorization is a difficult challenge. On the other hand, it can be one of the most useful and rewarding memory feats you can achieve. Thankfully, there are several methods that make memorizing easier, and we'll learn more about those in this chapter. But first let me introduce you to two people who have made some interesting discoveries about memorization.

The first is my son-in-law, Larry. Larry has an amazing memory for almost everything—everything except lyrics and text that is. Larry can remember the games he played in nursery;

he can even remember his mother pinning on his diaper. Most people cannot remember anything before their third or fourth birthday.

As a computer programmer, Larry can remember, coordinate, and integrate dozens of lines of programming language on two screens at once. He's an accomplished musician and can play four or five instruments all by ear—not at the same time, of course! He does have some limitations.

Larry also knows dozens, if not hundreds, of musical arrangements by heart. He can listen to a concert and identify the music of each of the instruments. However, what he cannot do well is remember lyrics. He claims his brain gets so into the music that he cannot focus on the words. He also struggles with memorizing text of any significant length. However, being a bright guy, he's figured out a few ways to overcome this challenge.

Not-So-Vain Repetition

For many years Larry avoided memorizing words because it was difficult for him. Indeed, he feels he developed a mental block against memorization. And when he was forced to, like when he had to memorize the lyrics of a new song for his band, he did it purely by rote, and it took him an inordinate amount of time. Then, he started studying artificial intelligence and gained insight into how the brain works. He reasoned that if computers could learn by having material repeated over and over, he must be able to do this as well.

His basic method, after that, did not change a great deal. He continued to memorize by rote, repeating the material over and over. He would learn a small chunk, then add a bit more, repeat the whole thing, add a bit more, repeat all of that, then add a bit more. He did this over and over again. But he found he was able to retain it much faster. Why? Because he had realized that if a computer could learn through repetition, then his brain must also be able to pick up more than he had previously thought.

Larry had learned that there was such a thing as unvain

repetition. In other words, he realized his repetition was not in vain. It was, in fact, producing tangible results. Consequently he began to trust his brain more, and the more he trusted his brain, the better it got.

His experience reminds me of the admonition in Doctrine and Covenants, section 88, to "seek learning, even by study and also by faith" (v. 118). It's important, as my son-in-law learned, for us to trust and have faith in the ability of our memory. If you think you can't memorize, you probably will have a difficult time, but if you expect your brain to deliver, it usually will.

This is reminiscent of Henry Ford's purported observation that if you think you can do a thing or think you can't do a thing, you're right.

John Memorizes the Sermon on the Mount

One of my good friends has acted out the role of Jesus in various plays. More recently, he decided to perform the entire Sermon on the Mount. He told me that this was much harder for him than playing a role in a play, where you can cue off other actors to help you remember your lines. In this extraordinary feat of memory, John learned three chapters—more than four double-column pages of text—which took more than thirty minutes to deliver nonstop. If you don't think that is a lot, try it some time. One of the things that makes this even more amazing is that John has dyslexia—a learning disability that makes it hard for him to read and retain what he's read.

I asked John how he did it. He acknowledged that it wasn't an easy task; it had taken him many months. But he learned several things in the process that made it easier as he went along. He just wished he had known those things at the beginning because it would have saved him some time. I think you'll find his methodology insightful. As you read his process, you may want to jot down the various principles and techniques he used that we have already discussed, in addition to any new ones that you see.

First, John read the text over and over.

Second, he meticulously recorded on audiotape every verse, phrase by phrase, making sure he had just the right inflection in his voice. He wanted to make sure he had a good audio copy of the text, letter-perfect just as he wanted it delivered, without errors. He recorded this four times onto a single tape, twice on the front side and twice on the back.

Third, he played the tape on a tape player that played continuously, automatically switching from one side to the other. The tape played in the background throughout the day as he pursued his normal, everyday activities.

Fourth, he wrote down as much of the text as he could from memory. He wrote it over and over again. He later told me that for him, this was the most helpful technique. He felt that this really helped drive those lines deep into his memory.

At places where he got stuck, he would write out a key phrase to begin the next thought, like "blessed," to help him remember the beatitudes. Then he wrote out each of these blessed statements:

- Blessed are the poor in spirit.
- Blessed are they that mourn.
- Blessed are the meek.

He would first write and then read and recite each phrase fully. Then he would block out some of the details and try to recite the same thing again.

Fifth, he drew some cues or icons for himself, first in the text and then in sequential order on a separate sheet of paper. These were picture cues to remind him of the text, such as a flower for "lilies of the field," a candle for "let your light so shine," a gavel for "judge not," and so on. He then practiced reciting the text using just his icon list.

Sixth, he envisioned Jesus delivering the Sermon on the Mount, with props that may have been available to him—lilies, birds, the meek, the poor, and so on. John noted that as he went through this step, he would ask himself, "What is being taught here?" He found as a result of this that he was able to see more clearly the logical flow of the sermon and story line. He was able to see how concepts such as judging and forgiving tied together, and the whole thing began to make more sense to him.

Seventh, he delivered the lines vocally to himself and then with live props, which were similar to his icons. For example, as he went through the sermon, at appropriate times he picked a flower, touched a thistle, held up a beam to his eye, and pointed to birds in the air. He also incorporated different body movements to go along with the words. He noted the importance of giving appropriate emphasis, inflections, and expression when stating his lines, and giving the same emphasis or inflection each time he rehearsed. He said he got this idea from music and songs, which are easier to remember because of the rhythm and inflections. These inflections added audible but consistent variety to the text, which made it easier to remember, especially for a person with an auditory preference.

One other thing John did to improve his delivery and make it more memorable was to videotape his presentation. Not only did this help him identify ways to improve, but it also helped to burn a deeper, more memorable audiovisual image into his brain.

Additionally, he noted that he didn't try to tackle this all at once. He took one section at a time. First the Beatitudes, one thought or idea at a time, and usually not more than five verses a day. He also explained that he reached a point in chapter 6 when his brain seemed to "turn to mush," and all the verses became jumbled together.

At that point, rather than trying harder to unscramble it, he simply put it away for three or four weeks. When he came back to it, his subconscious mind had put everything back in order again. He felt his brain simply got overloaded and needed time to regroup.

So that's how John did it. And he did an amazing job in his live outdoor performance, I might add.

Now, let's see how many principles and techniques John used that we have covered. How many did you note? I found twelve; you may have identified even more. This is my list:

First, John used all seven basic principles in the A RECORD formula. He read each section, paying close *attention* and getting involved not only with the words but also with the themes, the concept flow—what was being taught—and the voice fluctuations. He *related*, or associated, different elements in the text to various symbols he was familiar with. He *envisioned*, or visualized, the key words, the icons, the setting, and Jesus delivering it. He used *concrete* visual aids like icons and even real props.

Finally, he found that it was helpful when he was able to see the order, or *organization*, in Jesus' sermon. John also organized his icons chronologically. He obviously had many *rehearsal* sessions. And not only did he envision and practice *delivering* this famous sermon to others, but he also provided several performances, which no doubt deepened his memories even further.

He visualized and engaged in action and interaction as he envisioned and then enacted Jesus' sermon using the available props and people. He used iconic symbols that he created and drew himself. He also wrote out the script. And he involved other senses as well, especially auditory.

In addition to what I have in previous chapters, John organized his material and practiced it using only his icons. He placed props or cues in his environment to prompt or remind him along the way. He also incorporated body movements such as pointing to the flowers and birds, and he used voice inflections to go along with the words. And when his brain got overloaded, he simply gave it a rest. And although I didn't mention it, I'm sure John did a lot of praying for assistance throughout this process.

Now can you think of anything else that may have helped John accomplish this even faster?

One thing that comes to mind is mental mapping. John may have gotten a faster start had he developed a memory map of the entire sermon, or at least each significant part, using key words and symbols. Then he might have focused a bit more on visualizing links or concept connections. This may have given him the sense of order or organization in the sermon that he noted was very helpful but that he didn't actually pick up until months later.

However, John did an outstanding job, especially considering that he was figuring this all out for himself, without any memorization books or guides.

Additional Tips and Techniques

An extension of the idea of adding inflection would be to add rhythm, rhyme, or music, much like the rhymes many of us learned to memorize the number of days in each month (*Thirty days hath September, April, June, and November* . . .), the ABCs, or the books of the New Testament. If you have a musical mind, these can be very helpful, as well as entertaining, to develop. (See *The Children's Songbook* for songs on the Old Testament.)

Scriptural verses, however, are usually not as easy to put to song because most songs have lyrical or rhyming words, which Bible verses do not usually have. However, any type of interaction with text requires your attention and involvement, which usually makes learning easier and more memorable.

Overcoming Mental Blocks

One of the keys mentioned by Larry, my son-in-law, that helped to improve his memorization was a change in his self-talk and self-concept. As long as he told himself he had a poor memory for lines or lyrics, he did. But when his new insight enabled him to change his self-perception or concept regarding his memory, he found his ability to recall improved dramatically and automatically. This illustrates the power of the self-concept.

The truth is we all have far greater capacity for learning and remembering than we realize. The problem is that most of us have imposed limitations on our memory. In a sense, we have been brainwashed by a few bad experiences into believing that we are far less capable than we truly are. One of the things that hypnotists do is remove these self-imposed barriers and set their subjects free to achieve more of their true potential.[1]

We usually don't need a hypnotist, however, to achieve this liberation. In fact, studies on this topic suggest that what we say to ourselves is often more powerful than what a hypnotist or some other person might instruct us to do. That is why watching our self-talk is so important for good mental health.

If we tell ourselves things like, "I won't remember this," "I can't recall that," or "I simply don't have a good memory," we are brainwashing ourselves into believing that self-limiting garbage. If any of those phrases sound familiar to you, then you need to start using more liberating affirmations.

There are actually two parts to making effective affirmations. The first consists of expressing our desires as if they had already been achieved, in a positive, affirming manner. The second is catching ourselves behaving in accordance with these desires—in essence, affirming to ourselves that what we are saying in our affirmations is true.

Effective affirmations of the first kind have three qualities:

- They are stated in the first person—"I am . . ."

- They are stated in present rather than future tense, as if they were already true.

- They are infused with positive emotion or expectation, again, as if this had already been achieved.

It's apparent that the subconscious mind tends to respond in accordance with, and actually perpetuates, what it believes to be true. In this regard, it acts much like a thermostat to keep us in balance. So whenever our behavior falls outside of the constraints of our self-concept, our subconscious mind tends to pull us back in line.

This can be useful in maintaining our integrity and helping us live in accordance with our highest values and within the behavioral boundaries which the Lord has prescribed. That is true and helpful when we believe ourselves to be good, and when we genuinely believe in our own divine potential. It becomes dysfunctional, however, when we believe we are less capable than we truly are. In either case, it appears that our self-concept, based upon our self-talk, will tend to perpetuate what it believes to be true now, not what we wish were true in the future.

Therefore, whenever you make up your affirmations, make sure that they are stated as if they were true, or becoming true, in the first person. Ideally, these affirmation should be stated with some emotion and conviction.

Now a word about appropriate emotion—and then on to some affirmations. What emotion would you feel if you suddenly found that you had a terrific memory for anything you had ever read and wanted to remember in the scriptures? Would you be happy, glad, excited, enthused, exuberant? Any of these emotions will be helpful as you make your positive affirmations. However, it might serve us well to remember gratitude. Appreciation for what we have and enjoy is not only one of the most important emotions to feel but also a catalyst to other good things. The Doctrine and Covenants suggests that the Lord delights in blessing those who are grateful, who acknowledge His hand and the blessings already received in their lives.

So following these principles and simple guidelines, here are some affirmations you may want to consider using to improve your memory. Keep in mind, however, that these are only suggestions. As with the memory-enhancing images, the ones that will likely work best for you are the ones you come up with on your own.

- I have a great memory.
- I am able to remember more of what I read each day.
- I practice the seven habits of highly effective learners.
- I vividly visualize the things I am trying to learn.
- I create concrete images to represent what I read.
- I organize the material I read to make it more memorable.
- I pay attention to things that are important to remember.
- I create vivid associations between new material and familiar images.

- I create powerful mental images for later recall.

- I enjoy mapping new information for total recall.

- I remember well the things that I imagine.

- I can clearly visualize the things I read and hear.

- I periodically rehearse the things most important to remember.

- I repeat these affirmations daily.

- Each day I'm getting better at applying the things I've learned.

- My memory is improving dramatically.

The next step in using positive affirmations is to notice that any time you see one of these affirmations occurring in your life, you say, "Yes, this is becoming more and more my reality!" You don't want to wait for the big "aha's" to do this. The secret is to catch yourself doing the small stuff. Catch yourself making clear concrete mental images and say, "Yes! I'm doing it." Whenever you map a chapter or memorize a verse, praise your achievement and note, "I'm getting the hang of this, and it's becoming much easier for me."

Whenever you tie text to a memory peg in a creative or memorable manner, affirm your increased abilities. And whenever you remember to affirm your small achievements and progress, praise and affirm yourself for remembering to praise and affirm yourself! You can say, "See, I'm getting into the habit of this affirmation stuff, and my memory is definitely improving!"

Interestingly enough, this concept is reminiscent of an idea that Alma teaches in the Book of Mormon. If you check out Alma 32, you will see that this process is much like planting and nourishing seeds of faith. Indeed, in making affirmations you are exercising faith that your memory is improving. And like planting seeds in a garden, affirmation must be planted in the fertile soil of your mind. Then if you water them, by continuing the affirmations, catching yourself behaving accordingly and weeding out any sprouts of doubt, you will begin to see the fruits of a better memory unfolding before your eyes. And this faith will begin to expand and enlarge your memory, and the fruit thereof will be delicious to your taste. Enjoy!

Notes

1. Although hypothesis is not required to affect this process and expand your capabilities, if you find that these affirmations alone cannot change your self-concept or get you past your prior mental blocks, you may want to consult with a psychologist, psychiatrist, or good hypnotist. If you feel that you have more organic problems such as poor circulation or age-related cognitive decline (ARCD), you should see your doctor. Often a relatively minor and easily corrected circulatory or vascular problem can make a major difference.

9

PUTTING IT ALL TOGETHER— THE APPLICATION

This chapter is perhaps the most important! All the other chapters prepare us for this one because if we can't put all these principles, methods, and strategies together to help us remember what we want from the Old Testament, of what value are they?

You'll notice that I share a lot of personal insight and experience in this chapter. This doesn't necessarily mean you need to do everything I do. Some of these activities and formats may not work for you. These ideas and suggestions are to help jump-start your brain and help you apply the principles and methods contained in this book. You likely will come up with some better procedures than I have. When you do, please share those with me and others on my website at www.arecord4lds.com. That's part of the plan, as I understand it, to "instruct and edify each other" (D&C 43:8) for our mutual edification and progression.

The first thing we need to do to apply these methods to our gospel study is decide what's most important for us to remember. I realize this book is titled *How to Remember Everything in the Old Testament*, but that was just to get your attention. Now that you're three-quarters of the way through the book, you probably realize you're not going to remember *everything* (especially if you interpret *everything* to mean every verse) from the Old Testament. At least not in this lifetime! Memorizing takes time, and there's the rub. As I noted in chapter 6, there's simply too many more important things to do in this life.

However, if you interpret everything to mean every principle or teaching in the Old Testament that's important for you and your family's salvation and progression, then yes! By following the methods and principles taught in this book, that is quite doable. Just remember that since we don't have all the time in the world, and we do have other things to do, we must be selective.

As I'm reading through the Old Testament, or discussing it in class, I try to be on the lookout for ideas that seem uplifting or, as Paul put it, "profitable for doctrine, for reproof, for correction, for instruction in righteousness" (2 Timothy 3:16).

When I filter this guideline through my brain, I consider myself and family first, then those I have a stewardship over, and then friends of other faiths who may interpret doctrine differently than I do. Having had many discussions with them, I have a good understanding of those differences, so I'm always on the lookout for verses that tend to validate our beliefs.

The other criterion I use is to identify those verses or stories that seem to be impressed upon my heart. In other words, I believe the Spirit is telling me to pay attention to these concepts and ideas. Frequently, of course, these verses seem to fit into one of Paul's categories as well.

On this topic, Elder Henry B. Eyring counseled, "Since what

we will need to know is hard to discern, we need the help of heaven to know which of the myriad of things we could study, we would be most wise to learn. It also means that we cannot waste time entertaining ourselves when we have the chance to read or to listen to whatever will help us learn what is true and useful."[1]

Elder Eyring was speaking at a Church Educational System fireside, so his counsel was aimed at full-time students. However, it has relevancy for all of us. We all need the help of heaven to know which of all the things we could study, we should study.

Using these criteria, I haven't chosen to remember much from the Songs of Solomon. There's just not too much there that I find of use, either for doctrine or reproof. On the other hand, I have taken the time to either memorize, map, link, or peg most of Proverbs because it has much that fits Paul's and Elder Eyring's criteria. I would suggest first prayerfully setting criteria for what you want most to remember, and let the Spirit be your guide.

Next, for important stories, especially those with a major moral point, I try to key in on the most important elements. I sometimes include myself in the story and use vivid, sensory-rich imagery to visualize the interactions. Fortunately, stories are fairly easy for most of us to visualize and remember. And with multisensory imagery (seeing, hearing, touching, smelling, tasting), these stories become even more memorable.

If the stories are complicated or have numerous important elements, I may use linking techniques. If I'm teaching a lesson or have some other reason for including more extensive story or chapter details, I may map the scene or chapter. If the chapter contains key verses that I want to be able to refer others to, I peg the main ideas to the book and chapter number. If I want to be able to quote it, I copy it down and memorize it (see chapter 8).

For stories with multiple points that I want to have a good grasp of, as well as other important sermons or doctrinal chapters, I develop my own abbreviated script, utilizing key words and symbols from the text. I tie the opening text or first important concept to the peg word representing the chapter number. I then select the key elements of the story or sermon and write these down with essential supporting details, thus creating my own memorable mental pictures or movies of these important events and teachings. Having thus identified the critical concepts and created memorable symbols and associations, I tie them all together into a few paragraphs.

Generally I use the digitized scriptures provided by the Church for computer use. I usually read through the chapter and summarize the story, or supporting points. I often copy the key or desired text into my word processor and then cut out the chaff—the nonessential words or repetitive verses. I then add in chapter pegs, to identify where the most important teachings can be found, and other "enhanced" images, if not already included, to make the text more memorable. However, I place my memory pegs and other artificial elements in brackets so as to distinguish them from the actual biblical text.

Here is an example from 2 Kings 6, the miracles of the Prophet Elisha:

(I see two kings standing on the banks of the Jordan, each with one foot in one large shoe—6. Between them, floating in midair, is an ax head, and surrounding them in the air are chariots of fire.)

The sons of the prophets complain to Elisha that they do not have enough space where they are living. They suggest traveling to the Jordan to cut down trees to build there, and they ask Elisha to go with them. He does. While working, one of the sons loses a borrowed ax head into the river. Elisha cuts off a stick and throws it into the water, and the iron ax head rises and floats on the water, where the young man is able to pick it up.

At this same time, the king of Syria is warring against Israel and making plans to attack. Elisha discerns this and sends word to the king of Israel to avoid a certain area. Consequently, the Israelites double their guards in that area, and tell everyone else to avoid the area. Enraged, the king of Syria thinks one of his men has betrayed them. Then one of his men informs him, "Elisha, the prophet, tells the king of Israel the words that you speak, even in your bedroom." The king sends a mighty army to capture

Elisha. The men come in the night and surround the city where Elisha is.

> And when the servant of the man of God was risen early, and gone forth, behold, an host compassed the city both with horses and chariots. And his servant said unto him, Alas, my master! What shall we do?
>
> And [Elisha] answered, Fear not: for they that be with us are more than they that be with them.
>
> And Elisha prayed, and said, Lord, I pray thee, open his eyes, that he may see. And the Lord opened the eyes of the young man; [and the two kings with their foot stuck in the one large shoe] and he saw: and, behold, the mountain was full of horses and chariots of fire round about Elisha.
>
> And when [the army of Syria] came down to him, Elisha prayed unto the Lord, and said, Smite this people, I pray thee, with blindness. And he smote them with blindness [so they could not see their surroundings] according to the word of Elisha.
>
> And Elisha said unto them, This is not the way, neither is this the city: follow me, and I will bring you to the man whom ye seek. But he led them to Samaria.
>
> And it came to pass, when they were come into Samaria, that Elisha said, Lord, open the eyes of these men, that they may see. And the Lord opened their eyes, and they saw; and, behold, they were in the midst of Samaria.
>
> And the king of Israel said unto Elisha, when he saw them, My father, shall I smite them? Shall I [kill] them? (vv. 15–22)

Instead, Elisha instructed him to feed the soldiers and release them. So they had a great feast and then they returned to their master. And these marauding bands of Syria never returned to the land of Israel.

You will note that I've condensed, altered, and added a few

things to make it easier to read and remember, while preserving key elements. The King James Version of the Old Testament, being an old English translation of a much older Hebrew text, is sometimes written in, to our ears, rather awkward wording. Having been raised with this version of the Bible, I'm familiar with it. However, I also use the New American Standard Version at times for easier reading or to compare wording; sometimes it is clearer. I particularly like using it for Psalms and Proverbs, since it seems to retain the poetic style better.

I also find the footnotes, Bible Dictionary, and Joseph Smith translation helpful; these are included in the LDS edition of the King James Version. I may even include information from commentaries if they add significant value in understanding the story or concepts. I also include verse numbers for key passages. (Go to www.arecord4lds.com for examples adapted from the book of Proverbs that I use to help me remember the value of wisdom and whom she visits.)

I then record each scripture onto an audiocassette, which I play as I travel to and from work. I copy the verses I want to memorize to an electronic file on my computer. These files are set up as described in chapter 3 under the Rehearsal Principle and in chapter 6 under remembering names. I've included a sample here.

I've created these tables to fit in my day planner so I can review them when I have a few extra minutes. I can also remove a table and put it in my coat pocket when I don't carry my planner, or I can use it as a bookmark when studying the scriptures off-line. This way, I can easily add additional scriptures or notes as I'm studying.

To fit this page in my planner, I set it up in landscape format. The columns are made using the table tools available in Microsoft Word. When you create the table in this application, you can add text in one column, and it won't move the text in the other columns.

Outside	Inside left	Inside right
Concept, lesson, or quote	scripture:	clue:
For success—be not afraid or dismayed	8 Do all that's written in the law. Then thou shalt make thy way prosperous, and have good success. 9 Be strong and take courage; be not afraid, neither be thou dismayed: for the Lord thy God is with thee whithersoever thou goest (Joshua 1:8–9).	I see Joshua pick a tie [1] out of Moses' law book and use it to dress for success. Because he knows if he will do all that's written in the law, he will prosper and have success. He then bears the admonition: Be strong [I see him flex his bicep] and take courage [a lion on a leash]; be not afraid, neither be thou dismayed, for God is with thee.
Importance of revelation (vision) and goals	Where *there is* no vision, the people perish: (Proverbs 29:18)	I see a blind man lying on a hammock in my yard taking a nap [29]. An owl (Proverbs) is perched at the top of the hammock. I then see the blind man fade away into thin air.
God wants us to repent, turn, and live	God takes no pleasure in the death of the wicked. . . . Therefore, turn yourselves, and live ye (Ezekiel 18:23, 32).	I see a black dove [18] on a collision course with a geek's car. But then he turns away, turns white, and lives.

As I mentioned, at times I modify verses slightly to make them easier to understand and remember. However, I'm careful to retain the author's original meaning, although in translations, meanings are sometimes obscured. Of course, what you use for your cues is up to you. The important thing is that it makes sense to you and effectively reminds you of the verses to be remembered.

This is only one method that I have adopted. It works well for me because I usually carry my day planner with me. You may want to put your verses on 3-by-5 cards, with the concept or lesson on one side and the verse with cues on the other. I sometimes use these when I don't have my planner because they fit easily into a pocket.

As you can see, this system incorporates a variety of principles, learning modalities, and techniques to make sacred teachings more memorable for me.

Now you might think, "Wow! That's involved. That would take a lot of time." Yes, it does take time, usually fifteen to thirty minutes to prepare and write up my summary paragraphs depending on the length and importance of the story, sermon, or chapter. That's why I am selective. And it requires me to become involved with the message and text. But that time and involvement is one of the keys that unlocks this wisdom for application in my life.

How important is it to have a grasp of that iron rod at all times? Is it worth dedicating this much of your time and talents? As Jesus said, "For what shall it profit a man, if he shall gain the whole world, and lose his own soul [or that of a child]? Or what shall a man give in exchange for his soul?" (Mark 8:36–37). Is it not worth some time and effort to have this kind of eternal wisdom ready at a moment's notice, on the stage of your mind and the tip of your tongue, to help you and yours avoid the rising mists of darkness?

As Solomon said, "For wisdom is better than rubies; and all the things that may be desired are not to be compared to it" (Proverbs 8:11).

Additionally, I have found these personal scripts, tapes,

maps, and quizzes to be a good investment of my time. Although it takes time up front, now that they are made, I can review information quickly and easily. Plus, I can also review these during otherwise wasted time, such as driving or standing in lines. And I remember much more of what's important to me in the scriptures than I would if I were to only read for thirty minutes each day.

On this issue, Elder Eyring observed, "It takes neither modern technology nor much money to seize the opportunity to learn in the moments we now waste. You could just have a book and paper and pencil with you. That will be enough. [Actually, if you apply what you've learned in this book, you may need less than that.] But you need determination to capture the leisure moments you now waste."[2]

Teach the Children—But When?

"And these words, which I command thee this day, shall be in thine heart:

"And thou shalt teach them diligently unto thy children, and shalt talk of them when thou sittest in thine house, and when thou walkest by the way, and when thou liest down, and when thou risest up" (Deuteronomy 6:6–7).

Perhaps the biggest benefit of this investment of time is that I now have this information available to me whenever I need it. I have found, for example, that family home evening and family scripture study are not the only times to teach kids. Dinner time and drives in the car also provide great opportunities to share scripture verses and teachings.

I've been gratified to see drug prevention ads recently advocating dinner time together as a key to drug prevention. The reason it works, of course, is because once kids get their mouths full, their ears are still open. And they're not likely to get up and leave until they are done eating! In addition, some studies suggest people can sometimes relax and discuss better if they already have something setting their jaws in motion—really. For whatever reason, dinnertime is usually a good time to share the lessons of life.

However, it's awkward to have to run and get your Bible and try to look up scriptures while you are eating. It works much better if you have the information stored in memory and can simply tell stories or share the most important ideas. I remember on my mission, a district leader summarized Doctrine and Covenants 82:10 by saying, "The Lord says he is bound and determined to provide what we need, if we will just do what he says." Not exactly a direct quote, but the small variation in the vernacular made it even more powerful.

Driving in the car provides another wonderful time for sharing and teaching. Our family lived in England for three years, and during that time, our chapel was about twenty miles away. Our children were teenagers at the time, and so we usually made the trip at least a couple times a week for church and Mutual. My wife and I found this was the best time to talk with our children. We asked about school and other things going on their lives; we discussed Sunday School lessons and other gospel questions. If they didn't like the discussion—we tried to keep things fairly light—they couldn't just leave when we were traveling at sixty miles an hour.

Again, you can't pull out your Bible while driving down the road, although your kids may be able to look up verses for you. Knowing what the scriptures say and being able to share gospel principles and ideas from memory comes in handy!

Additional Ideas for Young Children

Let me share a few more ideas for helping young children develop a love for and understanding of the scriptures. As most of us know, one of the best things we can do for young, preschool children is read to them, especially at night before they go to sleep. And, of course, some of the best bedtime stories are Bible stories. I can still remember the Bible storybook my mother used to read to me as I sat on her lap in an old rocking chair.

When my kids were small, we read Bible stories to them as well. As they got older and we got busier, we purchased a set of dramatized Old Testament stories. My son especially loved these. Each night he played a different tape, until he had heard them all. And then he started all over. He could quote some of the tapes verbatim before he was five. I recall one summer when he was a bit older, he attended a local vacation Bible School with other Christian children. His teachers were impressed how much this little Mormon boy knew about the Bible, especially when some of them didn't even think Mormons believed the Bible.

One of the best things you can do for your children is help them have good experiences with the scriptures. Children should receive praise and other positive reinforcement when they know and can share gospel stories at a young age. That can go a long way in helping a child develop a love for the scriptures, as well as a desire to continue to study and remember them, and hopefully apply those teachings in their lives.

Totally Useful Teachings—The Game

Some years ago when the Totally Useless Trivia games became popular, I rebelled. I asked myself, why doesn't someone come up with a game that uses totally useful information, so families could enjoy some positive benefits from playing a game, rather than wasting their time on useless stuff?

I started developing such a game. I never finished all the rules or produced the game, but I think the idea has great possibilities! Let me share what I developed with you. Perhaps you would like to play it with your family for fun and profit—mentally and spiritually.

I call the game "I Have a Question." Here are the rules I developed. All questions are placed in a pile or hat. One person from each team picks a question and states, "I have a question." The player then reads the question. The other team has to give an answer, preferably using one or more scriptures that address the question. The team receives one point for a good answer; two points if the answer includes a scripture, with at least three words from the verse, as well as the book it's in or the book's author; three points if the answer includes the chapter the scripture is in; four points if more than one scripture is cited that answers the question; and five points if a relevant scripture is quoted with fewer than four words missing. Of course, you can adjust the rules as you desire. The point is, the more you know, the more points you receive.

Ideally questions will be divided into groups so there will be questions on various topics. Possible subjects include parenting, dealing with others, handling personal challenges, avoiding temptations, making good decisions, and doing missionary work.

One nice thing about this game is you don't need others in order to play it. While more people adds an element of fun and gives you a chance to show off your knowledge, you can still benefit from playing it on your own. When playing on your own, you compete against your past performance to see how much more you can remember.

Playing with others, however, is best. Sometimes we learn better as we hear others try to remember information we are seeing. That's the "study helper" phenomena. As you may have witnessed, often the person assisting in test preparation learns the material better than the best taker. But whether you play this game on your own or in a group, it's a great way to learn to apply the scriptures, and it's a super method for rehearsal and scripture memory mastery.

Here are a few questions, along with the associated scriptures. You can use these to get started, but I suggest that you develop some questions and answers on your own. It's fun! Try it. And I can guarantee you will be pleased with the strides you make in your understanding and application of Old Testament stories, teachings, and principles.

What Old Testament scriptures or stories illustrate the necessity of planning ahead?	Genesis 2:4–5 Genesis 42 (regarding Egypt)
Does the Lord bless His covenant people who have been wronged or hurt by others?	Genesis 30–31 (regarding Jacob) Genesis 41:41 (Joseph) Daniel 6:27
What does it mean when it says man was created in the image and likeness of God?	Genesis 5:3
What Old Testament evidence suggests that God expects parents to direct their children to obey their parents.	Genesis 18:19 Exodus 20:12
Where does the Bible teach that we need to learn to control our temper?	Proverbs 14:17; 16:32 2 Kings 5:10–14
What evidence is there that we have the potential to become gods, or like God?	Genesis 3:22 Psalm 82:6
Abraham 3:25 says that before we came to earth, we understood that we would be tested to see if we would do all God commands us to do. Is there any evidence for this idea in the Old Testament?	Genesis 22:1

What evidence is there that Jesus was the Jehovah of the Old Testament?	Isaiah 43:14; 54:5 Zechariah 12:10
What evidence is there in the Old Testament that we lived with God before we were born?	Job 38:7 Jeremiah 1:5
What approach is helpful when dealing with conflict?	Proverbs 15:1, 18
Is there any Old Testament evidence that doing good to your enemies can be to your benefit?	2 Kings 6:22–23

President Heber J. Grant once said, "That which we persist in doing becomes easier to do, not that the nature of the thing has changed, but that our power to do has increased."[3]

The more you practice these study and memory strategies, the more powerful your memory will become and the easier and more enjoyable it will be for you to remember what you want, when you want, to share as needed.

Notes

1. Henry B. Eyring, CES fireside for young adults, 6 May 2001; CES fireside for young adults, 6 May 2001.

2. Ibid.

3. Heber J. Grant, *Gospel Standards*, 355.

10

FOOD FOR THOUGHT

I am not a doctor. The ideas, information, and suggestions contained in this chapter are not intended as prescriptions or as a substitute for consulting with your physician. All serious matters regarding your health require medical supervision.

In chapter 2 we talked about two different aspects to memory: natural memory, composed of organic gray matter; and memory procedures. We also discussed a variety of memory procedures and various ways to improve them because usually they are the weakest links in memory. Unfortunately, many people believe that they have a poor natural memory, or insufficient gray matter, when in fact their primary problem is they don't know how to effectively store what they see and hear. That is why I shared those procedures up front. As you implement the seven habits and associated methods, hopefully you will find you have a much better memory, or more capable gray matter, than you had previously supposed. You simply needed a bit of training and improved procedures.

On the other hand, there are a variety of conditions that can have a negative impact on our natural ability to remember. These conditions include age-related deterioration in the structures of the brain, oxidation, plaque buildup in the brain, some prescription medications, poor circulation of vital oxygen and nutrients, and degeneration in the supply of chemical messengers or neurotransmitters, particularly acetylcholine. Fortunately, there are many things that we can do to overcome these conditions and improve the quality and capability of our natural memory. In this chapter, we will talk about some nutrients and other measures you can take to support healthy brain functioning and keep your memory sharp and clear.

In chapter 2, we learned that the brain needs five things to function at its optimal capacity:

1. Healthy cerebral cellular structures

2. Neurotransmitters

3. Good nutrition

4. Plenty of oxygen

5. An effective circulatory system

These elements need to be performing their own proper functions and working in concert with each other, and not be inhibited by any other harmful substances, including drugs or medications. If any one of these elements is missing or seriously depleted, or if other substances are inhibiting proper function, we may experience some type of cognitive or mental deficit. Even a low-grade problem in one or more of these areas over time can result in memory storage or retrieval problems. In short, people struggling with these problems won't be able to recall what they want to, when they want to, even though they feel they ought to be able to.[1]

People may experience problems with their natural memory physiology for many reason, with the most common being vascular or circulatory problems. Therefore, it is always best to consult your physician or a neurologist if you are experiencing a significant decline in memory. Otherwise, you could waste a lot of time and money pursuing blind alleys when the light, in fact, lies at the end of another path. The nutrients described in this chapter, as well as strategies described in chapters 3 through 9 can prove useful in preventing or dealing with a wide variety of memory problems. However, the more you know about your specific needs, the better you and your doctor will be able to develop a program that is effective for you.

Helpful Nutrients

It was once thought that the brain was somewhat immune to nutritional deficiencies. We now know this is false. The brain needs more nutrients, including glucose and oxygen, than any other part of the body. When deprivation lasts too long, problems occur. For example, studies in every decade since the 1960s have found that children who do not eat breakfast are not able to concentrate and do as well in school as children who do.[2] Their brains simply aren't getting the necessary nutrients they need to function well.

Most healthy adults who do not have blood sugar problems are less vulnerable to this fasting phenomena. In fact, most adults suffer more memory problems from eating too *much* than from eating too little. Large meals draw blood from the brain and can often leave a person feeling tired and unable to focus. More frequent, smaller meals likely serve us better.

However, as we advance in years, our bodies begin to lose

some of the enzymes and other nutrients needed to break down and assimilate protein and other food that the brain needs to create neurotransmitters and the mechanisms of memory. Therefore, we again become more vulnerable to malnutrition and memory problems. A study of 260 Albuquerque residents over the age of sixty-five found that those with the lowest intake of various nutrients consistently scored lower than the rest in tests of memory.[3]

The primary food for the brain is glucose. About 30 percent of our daily calories are devoted to brain functions. The body can synthesize glucose out of various foods, but if a person doesn't eat much, their brain may become starved of this most fundamental fuel, as well as other necessary nutrients. In a study reported in the *British Journal of Clinical Psychology*, "women on very low-calorie diets displayed poorer reaction speeds, immediate memory and ability to sustain attention, compared with the women who were eating a moderate amount of calories."[4]

Of course it's not only people on diets who are vulnerable to starving their brains. Calories and nutrients can be lacking whenever we lose our appetites, whether it's from anxiety, stress, stomach upset, or generally not feeling hungry. At a care center where I once worked I noticed that we often began to see a decline in memory, or an increase in confusion, when a person started eating less.

So what nutrients are necessary for memory? All of them! This is why it is so important to eat a well-balanced diet including fruit, vegetables of various colors, grains, nuts, and seeds. These foods, especially in their raw, or unprocessed state (after a thorough cleaning to remove wax and pesticides) and *when taken in sufficient quantities,* appear to have all of the vitamins, minerals, enzymes, proteins, and fats that the brain needs to function well. And yes, I said fat. Most people do not realize it, but unsaturated fats or lipids are the primary building blocks of the brain. That's why a mother's milk is so high in fat, particularly DHA (docosahexanoic acid).

But, you might ask, "Where's the beef?" Doesn't one need an abundance of meat and dairy products to provide the protein and calcium the body needs? Certainly the brain needs some protein, as well as calcium, but probably the best sources of protein for an aging brain are soybeans, nuts, seeds, and sea greens, not meat or milk. While beef, pork, and lamb are good sources of high-quality protein and vitamin B-12, they are also good sources of saturated fat. It may seem paradoxical, but while unsaturated vegetable, grain, or seed fats are essential for adult mental health, saturated fats—the kind that turn solid when left to stand at room temperature—have the opposite effect. These fats often slow down mental functioning and, through oxidation, can even cause damage to brain cells. They also add unneeded cholesterol to arteries, which tends to raise blood pressure and restrict the flow of other nutrients to the brain.

In one study at the University of Toronto, researchers found that animals fed diets high in polyunsaturated fats, particularly soybean oil, learned about 20 percent faster than animals that were fed lard or only regular chow. They were also less likely to forget what they had learned, suggesting improvements in both short- and long-term memory. Red meats are also reportedly harder for the body to break down and, in large quantities, can divert enough blood from the brain to make one lethargic.

It's no wonder then that when King Nebuchadnezzar offered meat and wine to Daniel and the other three wise Israelites, they asked instead for foods made from vegetables, seeds, and grain. As a result, "in all matters of wisdom and understanding," they were found to be "ten times" better than all the other "learned or wise men" in his realm.

Personally, I am not a vegetarian. Having been raised on a farm with cows and pigs and chickens, I enjoy eating all of them, especially fatty bacon. But the above-noted research, as well as other studies, does suggest that Daniel and his friends knew what they were doing when they asked for pulse. And the Lord knew what He was talking about when He told the Saints in the Word of Wisdom to eat meat "sparingly" (D&C 89:12). Therefore, I don't eat much beef or pork anymore because I know they can impair my memory. While I still eat most types of meat, I realize that some are likely better for me than others.

Fish has long been considered a brain food. Not only is it a good source of protein, but the oil in most fish, especially salmon, mackerel, and tuna, is also an unsaturated source of omega-3 fatty acids, including DHA. These fatty acids are essential elements for brain cell membranes. That's one reason that breast milk is so high in DHA. Additionally, omega-3 fatty acids assist in breaking down the bad HDL cholesterol in our arteries. DHA is a primary phospholipid or structural component of cell membranes. If you don't care for fish, other excellent plant sources of DHA are flax seeds, sunflower seeds, soybeans, and blue-green algae. If you've ever wondered how fish get so healthy, or how Nemo and his father were able to find their way home, now you know. Fish feed on algae, and most algae is an excellent source of protein, vitamins, and minerals, as well as DHA. It just doesn't taste quite as nice as freshly baked salmon.

I have been studying and teaching about nutrition for the past twenty years. One fact that remains constant is that, while many nutrients have been isolated and can be purchased in pill form or taken in teaspoons, the ideal way to get these building blocks of life is through whole, unrefined, organic, nutrient-rich foods. Why? Because in this whole food form, vitamins and minerals have cofactors—trace minerals, enzymes, and other micronutrients—that help our bodies get the most out of our food. Therefore, it is important to enjoy a variety of nutritious whole foods—and not to overcook them. Cooking some foods is necessary since botulism, salmonella, trichinosis, and other diseases that come from uncooked food are not so good for either our bodies or our brains. In fact, cooking can even help unlock the nutritional goodies in some foods. However, on the whole, most of us overcook more than undercook. Most of us eat more processed and refined foods rather than fresh fruit or raw vegetables.

For example, do you eat more potato chips or carrot sticks? Carrots are an excellent food full of vitamins and minerals, while potato chips are basically saturated fat and salt, both of which can contribute to clogged arteries and starved brain cells.

Many scientists and nutritionists today believe that most of us do not get enough nutrients from our food. Were you aware that, based on research over the past decade, the Recommended Daily Allowance for many basic nutrients has gone up? With all of the pollutants in our environment, it seems our bodies need more of certain nutrients than previously thought to strengthen our immune system and keep us functioning in optimal condition.

Additionally, tests have shown that because of overfarming and a lack of crop rotation, many of our veggies are not as nutritious as they used to be. At a recent seminar, I learned that our air does not even have as much oxygen as it did one hundred years ago. Moreover, a higher percentage of our food is processed at higher temperatures than ever before. Plus, the artificial coloring, preservatives, sugars, and fats that are often added to these foods can irritate or stress our systems and supply less nourishment than our bodies were designed for. It is not surprising, therefore, that blood and spinal fluid tests performed on individuals experiencing memory problems often show a lack of certain essential nutrients.

Finally, it appears that once a problem has developed, it may take more than a maintenance dose of certain nutrients to get the brain back on track. It's not surprising, therefore, that some food supplements have proven extremely helpful in facilitating various cognitive or brain functions, including memory, in both children and adults.

Specific Nutrients for Memory

From a basic multifunctional building block perspective, some of the most necessary nutrients for the brain and memory are the B vitamins, often referred to as the vitamin B complex. These include B-1 (thiamine), B-2 (riboflavin), B-3 (niacin/niacinamide), B-5 (pantothenic acid), B-6 (pyridoxine), B-12 (cobalamin), folic acid, biotin, choline, and inositol.

The B vitamins work in concert with each other to provide a host of services necessary for digestion, assimilation, damage prevention, relaxation, attention, and memory. Scientists have long been aware that deficiencies in the B's can produce a variety of symptoms associated with Alzheimer's and dementia.

For example, B-12 and folic acid are necessary to form myelin, the insulating sheath that surrounds the neurons and enables message transmission. B-1 serves to protect this sheath from the damaging effects of alcohol, smoking, and aging. It also enables the brain to utilize carbohydrates for energy production. Deficiencies in B-12 and folic acid are often associated with depression and memory problems, as in the Albuquerque study noted above.

B-1 deficiencies have been shown to result in anxiety, irritability, confusion, aggression, depression, and poor memory.

B-2 is needed to produce antistress hormones, and deficiencies have been linked to mental confusion, sluggishness, insomnia, and depression.

B-3 has been shown to improve the memories of middle-aged patients 10 to 40 percent.[5] It also helps prevent anxiety, confusion, paranoia, and depression.

B-5 helps protect neurons and provides support for the adrenal glands, which help the body handle physical and mental stress. Low levels of this nutrient have resulted in increased tendencies to anger, low blood pressure, stomach upset, and physical weakness. It may also play an important role in the synthesis of acetylcholine, which is vital for memory.

B-6 is necessary for the synthesis of other neurotransmitters called catecholamines, which help keep us alert, optimistic, and facilitate learning. Deficiencies in B-6 can also lead to anxiety, depression, and in some cases seizures.

B-12 deficiencies are commonly associated with dementia; sublingual (under the tongue) supplementation has been shown to facilitate the learning of new material.

Folic acid aids in the production of several neurotransmitters including acetylcholine and serotonin. Therefore, a deficiency has been found to produce irritability, forgetfulness, mental lethargy, and depression. (Most antidepressant medications are aimed at increasing serotonin levels.)

Choline provides the raw material for the production of acetylcholine and has accordingly been found helpful for improving memory, especially when taken in conjunction with other B's.

In their book *The Brain Wellness Plan,* authors Dr. Jay Lombard, a board-certified neurologist, and Carl Germano, a clinical dietician, state, "We cannot overemphasize the importance of adequate B vitamin intake for a healthy nervous system and proper brain function."[6] They further note the best dietary sources for these nutrients include whole grain bread, cereals, pastas, and meat. They also suggest adding a complete B-vitamin supplement to the diet. The B vitamins seem to work synergistically with each other. To facilitate memory, these authors suggest doses of 50 milligrams per day, taken with or just before meals.

C, E, and Free Radicals

Previously, we noted that the brain has a tremendous need for oxygen. Although the brain contains only 2 percent of our body weight, it utilizes 20 to 30 percent of the oxygen we consume. Additionally, our brains need a significant amount of blood to carry this oxygen, as well as other nutrients, to all the regions of the brain. One of the problems with this system, however, is that with oxygen comes oxidation and free radicals.

Oxidation is what causes rusting. It's what causes an elastic to lose it's elasticity when left out in the elements for too long. It results in the brown pigment that discolors the uneaten portion of a half-eaten apple. On our bodies, the brown spots that we develop as we get older are said to be evidence of this oxidation process going on inside our bodies. Indeed, oxidation is a leading cause of aging, including an aging memory.

Free radicals, in the biological sense, are tiny unstable and incomplete molecules with a single electron. Free radicals are naturally produced during normal metabolism and immune function. However, like sparks from a fire, they can damage and weaken other tissues and cells they come in contact with by robbing them of their electrons. Free radicals can be extremely damaging to cell membranes, proteins, enzymes, and even DNA. They are, therefore, considered a primary player in the aging process, but more particularly in neurological degeneration due to the high rate of oxygen consumption in the brain.

Controlling internal oxidation and free radicals is currently a hot topic of discussion in Alzheimer's research. While researchers don't blame oxidation and free radicals for Alzheimer's per se, it seems they are critical factors in a chain of reactions that eventually result in brain damage, tangled cells, and the loss of vital mental functions.

Various things can increase the production of free radicals including stress, exposure to pollutants from automobiles, pesticides, radiation (UV light), alcohol, and various drugs. Illness, infection, inflammation, and other health problems, including diabetes, arthritis, and asthma also increase production of these molecules, as does LDL cholesterol and elevated blood sugar. Many stimulants and metabolic enhancers like caffeine and diet pills also produce free radicals, but so do eating and exercise to some degree.

Our bodies know how to deal with oxidation and free radicals. They do this through the use of antioxidants. Antioxidants are powerful little compounds that prevent oxidation and mop up free radicals. They are abundant in various foods, and some are referred to as flavonoids. Lemons are high in antioxidant flavonoids. That is why when you squeeze lemon juice onto the uneaten portion of an apple, the apple will not discolor as rapidly.

Vitamin C is a potent antioxidant. Studies have shown a direct link between vitamin C and memory. In one 1960 study of 351 students, researchers found that while lower levels of vitamin C corresponded with low levels of alertness, increasing plasma levels of vitamin C by 50 percent resulted in a 3.6 percent increase on IQ tests.[7] Citrus fruit, broccoli, peppers, and other dark-colored vegetables are good sources of vitamin C.

Vitamin E, another powerful antioxidant, has also been shown to facilitate a variety of cognitive functions and even slow the progression of age-related mental decline. Studies conducted in rest homes and care centers have shown that by taking vitamin E supplements, individuals experienced significant improvements in mental health. These improvements included a better outlook, more pleasant disposition, greater ability to move around, and better cognitive functioning on a variety of scales, including memory. In one blind, or controlled, study conducted in Finland, after only four weeks, nurses could tell with 80 percent accuracy who was taking vitamin E and who was not simply from the improvements they witnessed.[8] Wheat germ, unsaturated vegetable oils, seeds, and nuts are all sources of vitamin E.

Another reason vitamin E is able to produce such seemingly miraculous results is because of its positive influence on the vascular system. In other words, it helps to keep our blood system in good repair, so that oxygen and other nutrients are able to supply our brain's many needs.

Ginkgo Biloba

Research in Europe, and now in the United States, has begun to focus on other compounds that may prove even more powerful than vitamin E in preventing oxidation, quenching free radicals, and improving circulation. Likely the best documented at this time is the herb ginkgo biloba.

The October 1997 issue of the *Journal of the American Medical Association* (JAMA) featured an excellent multicenter study using double-blind empirical methods that showed conclusively that an extract of ginkgo biloba was, in fact, effective in helping to alleviate cognitive problems in the early stages of Alzheimer's and other forms of dementia.[9] Although there was little to no improvement in the control group, which did not take gingko, at least 40 percent of those in the ginkgo group experienced a significant improvement in their thinking and functioning abilities, including memory. In addition, Alzheimer's disease progress was at least retarded in another 20 percent. Moreover, no significant negative side effects were found from this treatment.

The primary way in which ginkgo appears to help memory is by facilitating circulation or blood flow to the brain. So if your memory problems are due to poor circulation, ginkgo may help. However, in addition, ginkgo is an antioxidant, a free-radical scavenger that appears to help reduce the damage and damaging effects of Alzheimer's disease.

A more recent study, however, did not find that ginkgo had much of an effect on healthy individuals. So while it may help prevent some degeneration, it may not do much to improve your memory if your organic memory is basically normal. Ginkgo may have a tendency to thin the blood, however, so if you are on any type of blood thinner or anticoagulant, you should consult your doctor before taking this herb.

Other Potent Antioxidants

Some months ago I visited a friend of mine who owns a health food store, and he told me of vinpocetine, another plant compound that he claimed is significantly better than ginkgo for improving memory and circulation to the brain. Vinpocetine is an extract from the periwinkle plant (*Vinca minor*), and "it selectively dilates the arteries and capillaries in the head area, which improves circulation to the brain . . . and may help improve memory."[10] It also reportedly helps increase brain cell ATP (adenosine triphosphate—the cellular energy molecule) production, as well as the brain's utilization of glucose and oxygen. So it apparently performs several functions that are important for the brain and memory. It's no wonder then that more than a dozen empirical (scientific) studies have shown vinpocetine to be helpful in improving both the speed and accuracy of natural recall abilities.[11]

Vinpocetine is reportedly used extensively in Europe to treat a variety of mental conditions, including cerebral insufficiency, aphasia (loss of the power of expression), apraxia (inability to coordinate movements) resulting from stroke, dizziness, inner ear problems including tinnitus, reduced visual acuity, insomnia, and mild depression, in addition to improving memory and learning abilities with minimal to no side effects.[12]

I guess the moral of this story is, if you are thinking of taking ginkgo to improve your cerebral circulation and memory, you may want to consider vinpocetine instead, since it appears to provide more avenues for possible improvement of natural memory.

The information I've read on vinpocetine notes that while some users feel improvements within the first few days, others may not see major improvement in the above noted medical conditions for months, if at all. Vinpocetine is reportedly best taken with food, as some nausea has been reported when taken on an empty stomach. And the improvements you see may regress if and when you stop taking the herb on a regular basis. However, it is generally considered safe for long-term usage and may be worth a try.

Vinpocetine is available at most health food stores or can be ordered online. Because vinpocetine appears to operate via some mechanisms that are similar to vitamin E and ginkgo, it likely will also have a tendency to thin the blood. If you are on any type of blood thinner or anticoagulant, consult your doctor before taking vinpocetine.

Because antioxidants are so important in preserving our internal systems, God has provided an abundance of them, in a variety of sources in our environment. In addition to vitamins C and E, ginkgo, and vinpocetine, some of the most powerful antioxidants include acetyl-L-carnitine (ALC), alpha lipoic acid, glutathione, n-acetyl-cysteine, selenium, carotenoids, pycnogenol, grape seed or fruit polyphenols, coenzyme Q-10, and tocotrienols. All of these have proven to be potent antioxidants, and most have shown at least some degree of effectiveness in preserving mental faculties.

Most of these antioxidant-free radical scavengers can be found in the foods we eat, or ought to be eating. However, if a person is not eating well, and oxidation appears to be taking its toll, all of the above can also be found in supplement form. When taking antioxidant supplements to facilitate memory, you should consult with your physician. While few side effects have been found in clinical studies, it is possible to consume too many antioxidants in pill form. Those familiar with this field suggest it's best to go with a variety at lower doses. It would seem prudent to follow the instructions on the label unless otherwise indicated by a physician familiar with these nutrients and the condition of your body. Most doctors, however, will not be familiar with all of the above, or all that follows. For further insights on dosages and references, you might encourage them to purchase a copy of *The Brain Wellness Plan,* by Jay Lombard and Carl Germano; *Mind Boosters: A Guide to Natural Supplements that Enhance Your Mind, Memory, and Mood,* by Ray Sahelian; or *The Memory Solution,* by Julian Whitaker.

Supplements to Increase Memory Messengers

Recall that the primary neurotransmitter for memory is acetylcholine. Years ago it was discovered that acetylcholine can be derived in large measure from choline found in lecithin. And studies conducted at the National Institute of Heath (NIH) showed that specialized choline supplementation can improve learning and memory in both normal and memory-impaired individuals.

However, studies using various forms of isolated choline or lecithin have produced only moderate or inconsistent results. More recent research has found, however, that it's not only choline that helps increase acetylcholine in the brain; phosphatidylserine (PS) can as well. In fact, PS may be even more important to memory than dietary choline. Of course, cells need sufficient energy as well as nutrients in order to communicate and form memories.

If a cell is damaged or in a state of disrepair, it will not be able to perform its required functions. Phosphatidylserine is one of the most essential elements needed, not only to protect against free radicals but also to repair and rebuild damaged cell membranes. Additionally, PS is necessary to metabolize brain fuel, or glucose. It's no wonder then that studies have shown supplementation with PS to be helpful in restoring healthy mental functioning.

In clinical trails at Vanderbuilt University School of Medicine, and in another multicenter study with over 140 patients, it was confirmed that PS was indeed effective in helping patients, even with Alzheimer's, to improve their memory, learning ability, and other cognitive functions. Those in the early stages of memory decline made better progress than those with more advanced conditions, but in those who did show improvements, the effects lasted even after treatment was stopped.

This suggests that PS does indeed effect repairs in the structure of the brain.[13] The good news about PS is that it doesn't take as much PS as choline to produce an effect. The bad news is it's not cheap. However, Lombard and Germano note the average person would not need as much as those diagnosed with Alzheimer's.

Another one of the newer antioxidants to hit the market that may also help to increase acetylcholine and improve memory is huperzine A. This traditional Chinese herbal remedy is prepared from the moss *Huperzia serrata*, which has been used in China for centuries to treat fever and inflammation. Although this particular compound does not appear to reduce fevers or inflammation, Hup A does seem to be a potent inhibitor of acetylcholinesterase (AchE). An esterase is an enzyme, which in this case breaks down excess amounts of acetylcholine, the primary chemical messenger for memory.

In addition to helping patients with Alzheimer's, Hup A appears to be of significant value for those with less serious memory problems. At any rate it appears to be safe and relatively inexpensive. However, because it is relatively new on the market, you will likely find that, as with PS, it is only available in health food stores.

Important Minerals

Antioxidants may do much to prevent damage to memory cell membranes and mechanisms, but they do not provide the other nutrients that the brain needs to function at an optimal level. The complex of B vitamins and vitamins C and E may get us off to a good start, but minerals may be even more important.

Calcium and magnesium are two important minerals essential for healthy functioning. While calcium is an important constituent of the electrical impulses used in cognitive communication, magnesium assists in the production of other neurotransmitters, as well as ATP as noted above, a key element in the production, storage, and transference of energy. And remember, the brain uses up a lot of energy. Because these two minerals are so important to so many processes, deficiencies are not uncommon in mature individuals. It's also important to note that the body needs vitamin D, the sunshine vitamin, in order to make the most of calcium, as well as another trace mineral called boron. In one study of an elderly population with cognitive impairments, many of the residents were found to be deficient in boron.

Other trace minerals such as selenium, copper, and zinc have also been shown to be important for a healthy, effective memory. These three minerals play important roles in the production and function of several neurotransmitters and enzymes related to memory.

I take a formula[14] with trace minerals in it daily, just to be sure, and if I miss a few days I can tell a difference.

Other supplements I have tried and found helpful include DHA, vinpocetine, and Hup A. I also take grape seed daily, as well as a multivitamin supplement containing the B-complex vitamins, vitamins C and E, and a low-potency memory formula,[15] which contains choline, DHA, and trace minerals. If I feel my head is congested or I have a bit of a cold or headache, I've also found that half an aspirin will help my memory. But a tall glass of water and a good long walk will usually do the same thing for me as well.

However, there's an important concept to keep in mind here. It's called biological individuality, which basically means that each of us is different. Just because something helps me, that doesn't mean it's going to do anything for you. So it comes back to what I said in the beginning: If you feel you have a problem with your natural memory ability, start out by going to see your doctor. Have him or her check out any medications you are on to see if they might be causing the problem, and then have a thorough checkup. It's hard to fix a problem if you don't know what's causing it. And with memory problems, you'll find there can be lots of different causes. Moreover, this approach can save you both time and money, and may even save your life.

Once you know what the problem is, you and your doctor can discuss alternatives. That is when you may want to share with him some of the information noted above to see if any of these may be useful for you to try. It should be noted that all of these are over-the-counter, unrestricted food supplements that you or anyone should be able to pick up at almost any good health food store, as well as many grocery stores. Moreover, none of the foods I've reviewed here are noted as having significant negative side effects when taken as directed on the label. So if you feel your natural memory is not as sharp as it could be, you may want to give one or more of these a try for a month or so, to see if they make a difference. But there are other things you can do as well to improve your natural memory that won't cost you a penny.

Mental Exercise

As our baby boomer population continues to age, I'm sure we will find many more things that are important to keep our brains sharp and clear. But we already know a great many things we can do. Rather than give you another long list of things to do, I will just suggest a couple of things that have multiple benefits and then provide a few references for those with deeper interest.

In chapter 2, I talked about the importance of oxygen and

good circulation for the body and brain, particularly our memory. It's also important that we find ways to reduce the stress in our lives, and relax.

In light of that, it should not be a surprise to learn that one of the best things you can do for your body and brain is aerobic exercise. Aerobic exercise does all of those things for us. It increases nutrient assimilation—we get more out of the food we eat—and oxygen circulation to the brain, it reduces stress and helps your body to relax afterward. Physical exercise also stimulates your brain while physical inactivity tends to numb it.

Basically aerobic exercise entails any type of vigorous exercise that causes you to breathe extra hard for at least twenty minutes. So jogging, biking, swimming; a good hard game of basketball, handball, racquetball, or tennis; hiking, and jump rope all qualify. But one of the best ways is simply to take a brisk walk for twenty to forty minutes. Brisk walking gets your circulation going, increases oxygen intake, improves digestion, is low-risk for accidents or injury, easily accessible, and easy on the joints. Furthermore, it seems to help rid the body of adrenalin and cortisol, the stress hormones. As a result, exercise, particularly walking, if done regularly, appears to have a soothing or calming effect on the nervous system, which tends to lower blood pressure.

I've found if I get writer's cramp, have a problem I'm stumped on, or simply need to get some new ideas or words flowing, a good walk with my pocket recorder is one of the best things I can do. I personally have found, like many others, that I think much better when I'm walking. I ran cross-country in college, and still do some jogging, but I don't often get that runner's high, or endorphin surge. Perhaps I'm too distracted worrying about my knees wearing out! In any event, running is not the best time for me to think. Walking seems to work better at getting my mental juices flowing and facilitating information recall. So if you want your mind to stay sharp and clear, consult with your doctor first and then try exercising vigorously for at least twenty minutes daily, at least five times a week.

What if you can't exercise? Perhaps you are confined to a

wheelchair or have some other condition that prevents you from walking briskly, such as an incredibly tight schedule or pressure-packed meetings in your Sunday suit. Well, you still have two options. First, there are exercises other than walking. I have a friend who is confined to a wheelchair, and he gets out and puts miles on his wheelchair, albeit a special chair, and enjoys a good workout. But even if you can't get out of the house or are confined to bed, there are exercises you can do like stretching elastic bands.

There are also isotonic exercises, which involve muscular contractions without movement of the involved parts of the body, such as clasping your hands and pushing them against each other. You can even do these in long meetings. Any physical therapist can show you a variety of these. They can help get your blood circulating, tone your muscles, and even increase your heart rate and breathing.

You can always practice the next exercise: deep breathing. One of the benefits of exercise is deep breathing. That alone can help improve circulation and oxygenation of the brain, and perhaps even weight loss. Yoga has interesting breathing exercises. Simply sitting up or standing against a wall and breathing deeply enough to lift your chest, holding that a second or two, and then exhaling fully to the count of seven, then repeating that for even five minutes will help—although longer is better.

If we are not getting enough oxygen to our brain, we will simply not be able to think and function as well as if we do. That's the bottom line. So remember to breathe! And when reading or working at the computer, remember not to stay slumped over for too long. Such a position can restrict oxygen intake and may hamper retention. At least every hour, if you are not confined, you may want to get up from your desk and get a drink of water. Most of us don't drink enough water. The body and brain need oxygen and water.

The final category of exercises is specifically for your brain. Even if you are totally paralyzed physically, like the great physicist Stephen Hawking, any type of sensory stimulation and deliberate thinking—reflection, envisioning, imagining, linking, recalling, calculating, and so on—seems to produce "an immediate increase in blood flow into the brain."[16] With that in mind then, some of the best things you can do to stimulate or exercise your brain and improve your memory are the exercises contained in this book. Developing those extraordinary and vivid images in your mind, linking them and developing a strategy for recalling all the books in the Old Testament, recalling the contents of chapters, pegging concepts to chapter numbers, memory mapping, memorizing, and playing the "I Have a Question" game all stimulate your brain. In addition, these activities do much to keep your mind and memory sharp and clear well into the later years.

For more information on mental or memory exercises, look for books on memory improvement in the psychology or self-improvement sections of your local library or bookstore. Four of my favorites still in print are *Brain Builders: A Lifelong Guide to Sharper Thinking, Better Memory, and an Age-Proof Mind;* by Richard Leviton; *Don't Forget,* by Danielle Lapp, a professor at Stanford University School of Medicine; *Mind Boosters: A Guide to Natural Supplements that Enhance Your Mind, Memory, and Mood,* by Ray Sahelian; and, of course, *Your Memory: How it Works and How to Improve It,* by Kenneth Higbee. For additional references and information on nutrition and exercises for the brain and memory, go to www.arecord4lds.com.

Notes

1. See chapter 2, "The Anatomy of a Great Memory."

2. See *Child Nutrition Policy Brief,* from the Food Research and Action Center, Washington, D. C., http://www.frac.org/pdf/cnnl.pdf for a review of recent studies on this issue.

3. James S. Goodwin, *JAMA* 249 (3 June 1983): 21, 2919.

4. Cited in *The Memory Menu, American Health,* May 1998, 62.

5. Cited in Julian Whitaker, *Boost Your Brain Power,* 10; and Richard Leviton, *Brain Builders,* 108, 215. This finding is also supported in adult populations by the Goodwin et al. 1983 *JAMA* study cited in note 3 above, as well as in a study by M. C. Morris et al. ("Vitamin E and Vitamin C Supplement Use and Risk of Incident Alzheimer's Disease," *Alzheimer's Disease and Associated*

Disorders 112, no. 3, 121–26).

6. Jay Lombard and Carl Germano, *The Brain Wellness Plan*, 71.

7. Aaron P. Nelson and Susan Gilbert, *The Harvard Medical School Guide to Achieving Optimal Memory*, 85.

8. Related in Roger Yepsen, *Your Guide to Lifetime Memory Improvement* (Emmaus, Pa.: Rodale Press, 1986), 28; and in *Maximum Brainpower*, ed. John Feltman (Emmaus, Pa.: Rodale Press, 1991), 139.

9. P. L. LeBars, et al., "A Placebo-controlled, Double-blind, Randomized Trial of an Extract of Ginkgo Biloba for Dementia," *JAMA* 278 (October 22/29, 1997): 1327.

10. M. Beth Ley, *Marvelous Memory Boosters*, 23.

11. Ibid.; see also I. Hindmarch, et al., "Efficacy and Tolerance of Vinpocetine in Ambulant Patients Suffering from Mild to Moderate Organic Psychosyndromes," *International Clinical Psychopharmacoloy* 6 (Spring 1991): 31–34.

12. Ibid.

13. L. Amaducci, "Phosphatidylserine in the Treatment of Alzheimer's Disease: Results of a Multicenter Study," *Psychopharmacology Bulletin* 24 (1988): 130–34; see also L. Amaducci, et al., "Use of Phosphatidylserine in Alzheimer's Disease," *Academic Science* 640 (1991): 245–49. Both are cited in Lombard and Germano, *The Brain Wellness Plan*, 72; see also Thomas H. Crook III and Brenda D. Adderly, *The Memory Cure*.

14. The solution is called Liquid Gold and is mined from an ancient Utah source rich in trace minerals. This company also carries "Trace Minerals that Taste Good." For more information, go to www.landofhealth.com.

15. Memory Magic, from Land of Health (see 14 above). Other nutritional formulas for memory can be found in most health food stores.

16. Leviton, *Brain Builders*, 250.

11

HOW TO BREAK BAD HABITS
AND OTHER APPLICATIONS

Be ye transformed by the renewing of your mind.
—Romans 12:2

This chapter contains a three-for-one special offer. With one simple technique, I will show you a method for (1) making the seven habits of effective learners an ingrained part of your daily life, (2) ensuring total recall of anything you want in the Old Testament and beyond, and (3) overcoming any bad habits. Moreover, you will learn how to do all three at the same time! All at no extra charge! And, oh yes, as an added bonus (as if this weren't enough), this technique will also enable you to reduce if not totally eliminate the influence of Satan and his demons in your life.

Some years ago I worked in a center that specialized in helping people overcome bad habits to extend their life. One day, while working with an LDS client, I felt inspired to suggest the following technique. The essence of this technique is reconditioning your brain so that promptings to perpetuate bad habits will cue you to cultivate a new healthier habit. But before I get into the details of this strategy, let's talk a bit about habits.

Every January for five years I taught a series of classes on how to keep New Year's resolutions. The class was called "Changing Course." One of the reasons I liked to teach the class was that I knew I needed it. As I noted in chapter 3, teachers learn more from teaching a class than the students who attend. And I always had one or two pesky bad habits I wanted to overcome. If I ever ran out, all I had to do was suggest to my wife that I felt that I was approaching perfection and *voila*, she instantly made me aware of one or two more issues that needed attention. Anyway, in those sessions, getting down to the nitty-gritty of changing habits, I learned the following:

• Behavioral habits are supported by thinking habits, or associations. Some habits are simply thinking habits or thinking behaviors, such as worrying, anxiety, fear, phobias, and depression. These thinking ruts can be very deep, self-reinforcing, often hard to self-identify, and, of course, hard to break out of.

• Substitution is a key to breaking bad habits. You can't just focus on stopping a habit. This will only cause you to think about it more. You must come up with a more constructive incompatible habit or behavior to replace it with.

• Some habits are perpetuated by the adversary—Satan—whose desire and design is to thwart our progress and see us miserable. And He is not to be underestimated. But . . .

• God can and will help us, even in miraculous ways if we seek Him in faith.

Since this is not a book on habit control per se, I'm not going to go into depth on the first two insights. If your habit is one primarily of thought control, such as anxiety or depression, what follows may help. However, I also recommend you read *Feeling Good*, by David Burns, M.D. And if your condition is serious, regardless of the nature of the habit, you may want to seek professional counsel from a psychologist or psychiatrist familiar with the principles of cognitive behavior therapy.

Regarding the third insight, when working on habits that affected people's self-esteem or spirituality, if I could recondition a client to respond to the same perverse promptings with a righteous action, instead of the former degrading or self-defeating habit, often those promptings would go away. It makes sense if you believe there are evil forces that can and do entice us to degrading or self-defeating behaviors, which I do.[1]

Think about it. If every time you were enticed or prompted to do or think something unrighteous or degrading, you instead allowed that prompting to remind you to do something good, uplifting, or for God. After a while, these demons might see the futility in their attempts and stop the promptings,[2] at least on that matter. And, in fact, I've found in many cases, this is exactly what happens. Or at least it appears so. I can't say for sure whether this is a spiritual phenomenon or a psychological one. All I know is that it usually works or is at least helpful. Moreover, it is in line with how Jesus responded to temptations.

The account of the Savior's response to Satan's temptations, as recorded in Matthew 4 and Luke 4, provides an excellent example of how we can overcome temptation.

"And when he had fasted forty days and forty nights, he was afterward an hungered. And when the tempter came to him, he said, If thou be the Son of God, command that these stones be made bread." The Savior responded, "It is written, Man shall not live by bread alone, but by every word that proceedeth out of the mouth of God" (vv. 2–4).

Notice that Jesus didn't just respond by citing scripture but rather by citing a scripture about the importance of scripture, thus making the point doubly strong. In fact, Jesus responded to all three temptations by citing scripture. This suggests that perhaps the best way to deal with temptation is to fill our minds with the word of God—scripture. If we do not have the word of God treasured up in our memory, we may not be able to properly respond when temptations arise. In other words, we oppose the temptations of passion, or the physical "natural man," with their opposite—the spiritual.

Now I will show how this approach can work with one of the major and most challenging plagues of our day—pornography. As I noted in chapter 5, pornography can be extremely addicting because of its chemical bond to memory. Pornographic images can effect the release of norepinephrine, which causes the brain to print the pornographic image deep into memory, making it easy to evoke and hard to get rid of. Pornography can actually stimulate a wide cascade of powerful chemistry, perhaps the most powerful that we have in our bodies because it is tied to essential elements necessary for the perpetuation of life. And as you are likely aware, once it gets going, this combined chemistry can be an extremely powerful, self-perpetuating driving force, leaving a person with a deep, almost insatiable thirst for more.

Unlike other appetites, this urge, once triggered, is not easily satisfied and doesn't easily subside. Even then, it doesn't take long to regenerate and begin its drive again, especially in a young, male body. The more we give into it, the more it demands as it drives a person toward reproduction or sins of biblical proportion.

For someone who is married, these passions can be an incredible source of enjoyment, can help draw a couple closer together, and can lead them to the sacred role of becoming cocreators with God. However, if the object of a person's desires is outside the bonds of matrimony, it can only lead to frustration or, worse, condemnation.

If you want to read the lamentations and pondering of a tortured soul who learned this lesson too late, you only have to read 2 Samuel 12:1–12 and the sad Psalms of David, particularly Psalms 6:6; 38:1–11; 17–18; and 88. No wonder David's son Solomon gave such stern warnings on the subject (see Proverbs

5:1–14; 6:24–35; and all of chapter 7).

So how can the seven habits help? Recall that the first of the seven principles of memory, reviewed in Chapter 3, is *attention*. We remember most and best those things to which we pay close attention. Unfortunately, in our environment there are many inviting cues (reminders, triggers, hooks) to catch a man's attention and make him vulnerable to further promptings from the adversary to pursue more of those images.

As noted, people who are addicted to pornography *often* experience very strong urges and promptings to pursue this addiction, to seek more and more explicit images, and in time perhaps even perverted images. One of the best methods to overcoming this habit is to avoid paying attention to it in the first place. In other words, we should avoid media (magazines, R-rated movies, salacious TV programs, and so on) that portray these provocative, eye-catching images. For women, this might not be movies or magazines so much as romance novels or daytime TV, which evoke mental images of licentious scenes. Obviously, the more we can avoid these in the first place, the less we'll need to deal with the consequences.

However, total avoidance is almost impossible in our society, especially when you walk through a mall and see ten-foot high window dressings or, more accurately, undressings; pass through a multitude of men and women who wear provocative clothing; and see obscene magazine covers in checkout stands and lascivious ads on TV. The triggers are everywhere, and nearly impossible to avoid all the time. However, remember what we said when describing short-term memory and the Attention Principle? Just because something is in our field of vision, we don't necessarily remember it unless we focus on it and pay attention to it for more than a second or two.

Also remember the displacement principle. If, after seeing an image, we can shift our focus to something different for more than a minute or two, that initial unwanted image will soon fade and be replaced by something else. And now we are getting closer to the method I want to discuss.

Sometimes we are caught off guard. Maybe we're pulled into a conversation or we inadvertently glimpse an image, and before we know it we are feeling an enticement to pursue—to look longer or ponder on something that we know we should not. This can even happen while reading the Old Testament. As noted in chapter 5, the Old Testament describes numerous scenes that would likely receive an R rating in a movie, especially if graphically displayed. Interestingly enough, such scenes and verbiage are not present in the Book of Mormon, even though they share a similar time period and language.

So what can we do when this happens? The key is in prior preparation. If you wait until you are in the midst of enticement to try to decide what to do, it may be too late—or at least harder. In other words, the sooner we turn away, the easier it will be. The key is predecision.

By predecision, I mean before we get into that situation deciding exactly what we will do. Dr. Richard Novacco developed this approach for dealing with provocations to anger.[3] He called it "anger inoculation." First, he would discuss with his clients the typical things that provoked them. Then he discussed appropriate alternative responses and had them decide on one or two that they felt would work for them. Next he invited his clients to get into a relaxed, comfortable position and have them picture themselves in a situation where someone would say or do something that would normally provoke them to anger. Once they could imagine this provocation, he asked them to take a few deep breaths, relax, and then imagine themselves making an appropriate response. Dr. Novacco had his clients practice this over and over with various provocations and responses. Thus, they learned to recondition their response pattern. So a previously provocative comment or action would now evoke a much more measured and appropriate response.

The same method can be applied to almost any bad habit or undesirable response pattern, from biting your fingernails to drug addictions, from thoughts of worry and anxiety to thoughts of depression. Our feelings and behaviors are almost always a result of our dominant thoughts and focus. If you choose to control your thoughts (and we all can with a little practice) and what you pay attention to, you can control, to a major extent, your feelings and your subsequent behaviors. The key is to choose appropriate familiar thoughts and replacement responses ahead of time. Then make sure you use the replacement response when the cues or triggers are encountered.

This is in line with the challenge of Joshua to "choose ye this day whom ye will serve" (Joshua 24:15). We must choose if we are going to follow the enticements of the adversary, the thoughts of doubt, worry, fear, lewdness, and so on, or follow the Lord in faith and focus on things that are virtuous, of good report, uplifting, or praiseworthy.

Every Sunday we are promised in the sacrament prayers that if we will always remember the Savior, we can always have His Spirit to be with us. As I noted in chapter 1, "How could anyone who loves the Lord commit a sin, if at the same time they are remembering Him?" It's highly unlikely. When I think of remembering Him, I believe that includes those things that He has taught in the scriptures. Are they not virtuous, praiseworthy, uplifting, and of good report? Indeed, as Paul noted, "They are able to make one wise unto salvation" (2 Timothy 3:15).

Steps for Mental Reconditioning

It's difficult, if not impossible, to simply stop a bad habit like smoking. The more a person tries by willpower alone to stop smoking, the more he will likely think about it. And the more he thinks about smoking, the more he will want to smoke.

The real secret is substitution. You've got to come up with and focus on implementing another incompatible habit in place of the habit you wish change. So someone trying to stop smoking would be wise to focus on developing better habits of exercise, perhaps deep breathing when tense, drinking more water and grapefruit juice, or eating more sunflower seeds. Then when thoughts of having a cigarette come to mind, these individuals use that as a reminder to think about how they are doing or what more they could do on those other habits. Or perhaps the words of some song that they like, or some scripture that will help them in their resolve, like, "I can do all things through Christ which strengtheneth me" (Philippians 4:13). Any challenging mental exercise, like recalling and reciting relevant scriptures, as Jesus did, will help.

Again one of the best strategies for overcoming any temptation and developing good habits is to recondition that temptation, so when it comes, it reminds us to review and do something good. Since temptations, enticements, and cues are everywhere, or at least are now frequently getting your attention, they provide a perfect reminder to practice what you have learned. If used in this way, the enticements of Satan can actually help you develop a better memory for the wisdom and truths taught in scriptures, or in other words, to get a better grasp on the iron rod.

Ironically, the primary reason readers choose not to apply the methods mentioned in this book is because they won't remember to apply these principles. Not being in the habit of studying in this fashion, most of us will simply slip back into our old read-and-forget mode. Thus, our old bad habits and temptations can prompt us to practice and implement these new habits of memory.

Clearly, the real key to distracting us from bad habits is to focus on something else that requires our *full attention* and the active use of our mental faculties. Therefore, reviewing or memorizing scriptures, or recalling lessons from the scriptures, is an ideal substitution. This is one of the most demanding mental tasks that we can undertake, next to creating those images, so they can be effectively stored in the first place.

Another argument in favor of learning and remembering verses from the scriptures is that these can provide wisdom that will help us deal more effectively with any daily challenges in life. As we're told in the Doctrine and Covenants, if we will "treasure up in [our] minds continually the words of life, it shall be given [us] in the very hour that portion" needed at that moment to deal with whatever temptation or problem may come our way (D&C 84:85). Pondering the scriptures will also bring the Spirit into our minds and hearts, which can further facilitate that process.

The following are a few of the many mental exercises or habits you can develop to shift your attention off things that are not uplifting and focus it on that which is praiseworthy.

- Try to recall what you last read in your daily scripture study.

- Try to recall scriptures you have previously memorized that increase your faith, courage, and moral strength.

- Practice reciting all of the books of the Old Testament in order.

- Recall to mind a memory map that you have constructed in as much detail as possible.

- Think of a challenge a family member is facing; then review scriptures you can remember and identify one that might be of help in this situation. If you have applied the method for remembering the location of scriptures, try to recall from memory where each of those scriptures is located.

- Think of someone else who could use encouragement, perhaps someone you home teach or visit teach, and try to think of a story or verse from the Old Testament that might help or encourage them.

- Carry around scripture cards of verses you want to memorize and peg to their location. Pull one out and work on memorizing it or developing a memory cue to help you remember its location in the future.

The Lord told Joseph Smith to "let virtue garnish thy thoughts unceasingly; then shall thy confidence wax strong in the presence of God" (D&C 121:45). These are all virtuous lines of thought, that can keep your mind from wandering into the paths of sin, frustration, and sorrow, while at the same time help increase your confidence and lift both yourself and others.

Confidence, or what the scriptures call *faith*, is critical. It can be helpful to remember that you are a child of God, with great divine potential. And furthermore, you have been given a special gift, that a member of the Godhead will be with you "withersoever thou goest" (see Joshua 1:9), if you seek the Lord. As you remember to apply these principles, you must affirm your progress, as we noted in chapter 8. As you do so, you will feel further increase in confidence and self-esteem, which will help to propel you on to victory and greater self control.

In review then, here's how you can use the principles and methods you have learned for improving your memory to help you overcome any bad habit or temptation, and to turn the enticements of the world to serve you in improving your memory for the scriptures:

1. First, identify the bad habit or temptation you wish to overcome.

2. Jot down those things that prompt you to think about or engage in that habit. Note thoughts and images you may encounter or that may come to mind, including things that others say or do that get you going in a destructive, depressing, or wrong path.

3. Note mental tasks or habits that you are trying to learn or develop. Ideally they will involve the scriptures. It's a good idea to write these tasks, or new habits, on a 3-by-5 card to carry around in case you can't remember them. In times of crisis, the faintest ink can be better than a flustered memory.

4. Find a time and place that you will not be interrupted. Get into a comfortable position, sitting or lying down. Then imagine being presented with one of those temptations. See yourself responding by shifting your focus to the memory task you are trying to develop. Take out the card if you need to, or go on to rehearsing the verses or building the associations you are trying to learn.

5. Practice this over and over at least daily for the first week. Each temptation and your more appropriate response or new habit pattern should be imagined at least three times. Then move on in

subsequent sessions to imagining other temptations or provocations, replaced each time by the response habit or memory task you are trying to develop. At the end of every session, it's important that you see yourself successfully overcoming the bad habit and developing the new good one. Then imagine how much better you'll feel about yourself when you have developed that response habit or memory task.

6. Next, practice this in live situations. Again, you may want to use your 3-by-5 card to prompt you initially, but in time the new memory response will become what is called a "conditioned response" or habit.

7. Finally, reinforce any positive progress you make. Tell yourself after every session, and particularly every time you respond appropriately to a real temptation, "I can do this! In fact, I just did! I'm getting better, and it's getting easier all the time." Then let your mind ponder the rewards that will come as you continue this behavior.

Caution: Satan is no dummy. Never underestimate his power or cunning. King David did, and he paid for it for the rest of his life. Satan will try to draw you back into your old habits in any way he can. Keep up and vary your practice. Then, "Pray always, that you may come off conqueror; yea, that you may conquer Satan, and that you may escape the hands of the servants of Satan that do uphold his work" (D&C 10:5).

If he gets the best of you on occasion and drags you back into your undesirable behavior, repent. Learn from the experience and get back on track. Self-recrimination, calling yourself names, and beating yourself up are usually counterproductive and can become disempowering tools of the devil. They tend to reduce our self-concept and make us even more vulnerable. Don't let Satan discourage you. Keep your eye on the end result, note the lessons in your notebook for future review so you can learn from your temporary slipup, and then move on with the program. (See Deuteronomy 1:21, 28–30; Ezekiel 18:30–32; Joel 2:12–13; 1 Nephi 3:7; and 1 Corinthians 10:13.)

Remembering to Remember

What if you are one of those rare souls who doesn't have any bad habits to replace? How can you develop other positive reminders to help you get into the habit of remembering your scriptures? How can you remind yourself to remember and trust in Christ, so that you might always have His Spirit to be with you to direct and guide you?

If you don't have enough outside influences providing cues for you, develop some on your own. And it's not hard. Remember, all your memory needs is a hint, a small cue or trigger to get it going in the right direction. Of course, you could make up big signs to post in prominent places that read: Remember to rehearse and apply your scriptures. Or: Remember Christ.

That could work, and may be the most effective. However, other simpler more versatile methods are also available. One of my favorites is dots. Buy or make colored dots that you can stick to things. Make a mental note that whenever you see one of these dots, you will think of Christ and review a scripture in your mind. Be sure to place the dots in places where you will see them during the day, such as on your bathroom mirror, your rearview mirror, the refrigerator door, or the screen of your computer.

If you do choose to use the dot system, don't ignore the dots. This too could become a habit, and then they will be of no value to you. It's better to respond to the dots as soon as you see them for at least three weeks. Respond to a dot by rehearsing a scripture when you first see it; then continue on with what you were doing. It's kind of like doing your home teaching by the first week of the month! You feel good that you've done it.

Once you've developed the habit, you can take the dot down or start developing a different habit with a different color. You will find that as you begin treasuring up on a regular basis the words of eternal life, your mind will "acknowledge [the Lord, so] he will direct thy paths" (Proverbs 3:5). I believe this is especially true if you take time to memorize Proverbs 3:5, as well as other similar scriptures, such as Psalm 1:1–3; Joshua 1:8–9; and D&C 121:45.

Remembering to Do Our Duties

In the first chapter I noted that sometimes we get so caught up in things, even good things, that we forget to do more important things—like keeping our commitments to others, fulfilling church assignments, and attending the temple. I know it can be frustrating to give assignments, count on people to show up, and then they don't. Of course, I have been the one who didn't show up at times! Maybe it's my experience with the latter, as well as my awareness of the fragile nature of memory, but I have come to the conclusion that when "active" members do not show up for assignments or events, it's not that they are rebellious, so much as they simply forgot. The simple fix? More tangible and appropriately placed reminders, cues we can't help but pay attention to.

Many of us simply assume that otherwise responsible people will remember these things. But without a reminder, and with so many other things going on in our lives, we don't. At work I use a day planner for all my appointments. However, I don't take that to church with me. In some callings, I had another binder, but I didn't always remember to review that when I should have during the week. So now I make notes on the back of our church bulletin and then transfer those notes after church onto our family calendar. This hangs near the telephone where we can easily review it throughout the week. Whatever method you use, it's important to develop a single method of reminders and use that one method consistently until it becomes a habit.

Now, I could develop a memory system for keeping track of these assignments and events in my head. However, for such transient tasks, I prefer the adage, "The shortest pencil is better than the longest memory." But you must also get into the habit of reviewing those hen scratches regularly.

Other common challenges are remembering our commitments to family members during the day or week. And akin to this is reminding ourselves of things we need to do during the day. Especially when we don't have a pencil on hand, or we think of something while driving the car.

Several memory tricks can assist with this sort of task. One of the simplest and most effective is tying a string on your finger. A variation of that is changing your watch from one wrist to the other; then, the next time you look for the time, you are reminded of whatever you associated with that change. I usually carry a comb, pen, and 3-by-5 card. If I think of something while driving, I hang the pen or comb from the front of my shirt. Then when I stop, I'm reminded and can write notes down. I also carry a small pocket recorder to record important thoughts and ideas.

If you have no method to write or record a task, you can use your memory and local cues to prompt you. For instance, imagine you are driving in your car when you remember that you need to call Mary to set up a time to plan Saturday's party. You also need to bake a cake for tonight and clip coupons for this afternoon's shopping. So you come up with a picture that contains all of those activities, and then you mentally tie it to something you will soon see in your house—like the door going into the house from the garage, the mudroom, stairs, or entryway.

For example, let's imagine entering your house from the garage. On the steps leading from the garage to your house, you imagine Mary, and she looks a wreck (to make it more memorable). It looks like she just stuck her face in a cake because her face is covered with frosting. She also has a pair of scissors hanging from her hair. Imagine this scene vividly. You might even imagine touching the frosting and licking your fingers to involve more senses. Then if your mind wanders to other things, as it usually does, when you arrive home and start walking up those stairs, that image will flood back into your mind and you'll remember to call Mary, make a cake, and clip those coupons. With practice, these memory reminders can be fun and have many different applications.

Go to www.arecord4lds.com for more practical tips.

Notes

1. See *The Screwtape Letters*, by C. S., Lewis for an interesting fictional, though insightful, treatise on how the devil and his demons work.

2. We could say that these evil enticements become purpose-defeating behaviors for them (the demons). If every time they try to tempt you, you respond with something uplifting, that defeats their purpose.

3. Richard W. Novacco, cited in the chapter on "Stress Inoculation" in Donald Meichenbaum, *Cognitive-Behavior Modification: An Interactive Approach* (New York: Plenum Press, 1977).

12

THE GIFT—LEST WE FORGET

In this last chapter, I want to briefly review the lessons we learned in the first chapter and discuss one more invaluable, even divine, aid to memory.

In chapter one, we reviewed how the Lord reminded Israel, over and over, of the importance of remembering that He had brought them out of bondage and remembering His commandments and their covenants. We reviewed the denigration and destruction that followed when they forgot these things, and the vital role memory played in bringing the children of Israel back to qualify for the blessings of their covenant. We also reviewed a few of the ways in which the Lord can and has reminded His people in the past.

Fortunately we who are members of The Church of Jesus Christ of Latter-day Saints have been given another gift to help improve our memories, so we do not need catastrophic reminders. Hugh Nibley, quoting Clement of Alexandria in the second century, notes that "Clement is aware, as Eusebius is, that the ancient apostles didn't need to write everything down because 'the blessed men of old possessed a marvelous power.'"[1]

This, of course, is what Jesus had promised them, that after His departure He would send the Comforter, even the gift of the Holy Ghost. And Christ promised that the Holy Ghost would not only teach us but would also "bring all things to your remembrance, whatsoever I [the Lord] have said unto you" (John 14:26).

Elder Spencer W. Kimball taught, "The Holy Ghost is a revelator. . . . He is a reminder and will bring to our remembrance the things which we have learned and which we need in the time thereof."[2]

Brigham Young noted, "The Holy Ghost reveals unto you things past, present, and to come; it makes your minds quick and vivid to understand the handiwork of the Lord."[3]

James E. Talmage was renowned in his day for having one of the sharpest intellects in the country. He observed, and no doubt experienced, that "through the influence of the Holy Spirit the powers of the human mind can be quickened and increased so that things past may be brought to remembrance."[4]

I remember my father telling me of an experience he had on his mission. He was giving a sermon, and his mind was "quickened." He taught things he couldn't even remember reading. Afterward he hardly remembered what he had said, but his companion testified that it was "a marvelous sermon." No doubt it was pulled from something he had read a long time before.

Elder Thomas S. Monson is another example of a modern-day prophet with an amazing memory. Who has not listened to him and marveled at his tremendous ability to remember stories, scriptures, poetry, and past events? Certainly he too is often aided by this gift and power.

Each one of us who has been baptized into the Church has been given this gift, but how often do we "receive" it and rely on its promptings to help us remember? Joseph Fielding Smith stated, "It is my judgment that there are many members of this Church who have . . . had hands laid upon their heads for the gift of the Holy Ghost, who have never received that gift, that is, the manifestations of it. Why? Because they have never put themselves in order to receive these manifestations. They have never humbled themselves. They have never taken the steps that would prepare them for the companionship of the Holy Ghost."[5]

So what are those steps?

Activating the Gift of the Holy Ghost

According to President Smith, one of the qualities necessary to receive assistance from the Spirit is humility. This seems to coincide with the admonitions of Solomon and Isaiah who taught, "Be not wise in thine own eyes" (Proverbs 3:7; Isaiah 5: 21). Those who think they know enough shall not be given more. In fact, they may actually lose what they have (see 2 Nephi 29:30). Some mistakenly equate humility with weakness, but a better biblical definition is a willingness to heed and learn.

In another sermon, Joseph Fielding Smith further noted, "The Holy Ghost will not dwell with that person who is unwilling to obey and keep the commandments of God or who violates those commandments willingly. That great gift comes to us only through humility and faith and obedience."[6]

This reminds me of Doctrine and Covenants 93:28 where we are told, "He that keepeth his commandments receiveth truth and light, until he is glorified in truth and knoweth all things."

In the vision of Joseph Smith to Brigham Young, we see similar counsel. President Young recorded that "Joseph stepped toward me, and looking very earnestly, yet pleasantly said, 'Tell the people to be humble and faithful, and be sure to keep the spirit of the Lord and it will lead them right. Be careful and not turn away the small still voice; it will teach you what to do and where to go; to keep their hearts open to conviction, so that when the Holy Ghost comes to them, their hearts will be ready to receive it. They can tell the Spirit of the Lord from all other spirits; and their whole desire will be to do good, bring forth righteousness and build up the kingdom of God.'"[7]

Humility, faith, and obedience appear to be important keys to activating this gift in our lives. But like any gift from God, it appears we must seek it. Jesus invited, "Ask, and it shall be given you; seek, and ye shall find; knock, and it shall be opened unto you" (Matthew 7:7).

After having sought this gift, we must, as Joseph counseled, be open, receptive, and responsive to its influence. Otherwise, it will not abide with us (see Mormon 2:26).

Some people may not believe the Holy Ghost can or will help us with our memory challenges. But if remembering is important for our salvation, as noted in chapter 1, then why wouldn't he? Perhaps we may feel our memory challenges are simply too mundane for him. And maybe many of them are. But remembering the scriptures? That seems important and very much in line with what Jesus declared the Holy Ghost's role to be. But again, if we don't believe or expect that, we probably won't experience it. It does seem to require some faith on our part.

Alma talks of cultivating faith in Alma 32. Try reading this chapter with the gift of the Spirit in mind and conduct a little "experiment upon my words . . . give place for a portion of my words." Plant the seed of faith in this gift in your heart. "If ye do not cast it out by your unbelief, that ye will resist the Spirit of the Lord, behold it will begin to swell within your breasts . . . [and] to enlighten [your] understanding" (vv. 27–28).

In a Church Educational System address in 2001, Elder Henry B. Eyring promised that "when we put God's purposes first, He will give us miracles . . . I know from long experience that He is faithful to His word." He then gave the following illustration of a time when he was in graduate school and also was given a major calling in the Church.

"I visited the tiny branches and the scattered Latter-day Saints from Newport and Cape Cod on the south to Worcester and Fort Devins on the west and Lynn and Georgetown on the north," Elder Eyring remembers. "I realize that those names mean more to me than they do to you. For me the words bring back the joy of going to those places, loving the Lord and trusting that somehow He would keep His promise. He always did. In the few minutes I could give to preparation on Monday morning before classes, ideas and understanding came to more than match what others gained from a Sunday of study."[8]

The apostle Paul, speaking of the gifts of the Spirit, encouraged us to "covet earnestly the best gifts" (1 Corinthians 12:31; see also D&C 46:8). Certainly, crucial teachings and counsel are two of those gifts. In section 88 of the Doctrine and Covenants, we are instructed to "seek ye out of the best books words of wisdom; seek learning, even by study and also by faith" (v. 118). Try it! Be humble, be faithful, and seek this gift in faith and prayer; see if the Spirit won't enlighten your mind, increase your understanding, and bring things that you have read to your remembrance.

Treasure It Up in Your Mind

As with all gifts of the gospel, however, the Lord requires us to do our part. Neither we nor the Spirit can draw water out of an empty bucket.

You may have noticed throughout this book, and particularly in this chapter, I have noted that different ideas or statements remind me of various scriptures. No doubt the same thing occurs with you. The reason for that, and the frequency of that, seems entirely predicated upon our prior study and storage. Because of the teachings and example of my parents early in my life, I developed a love for studying the scriptures. As a result, by using these methods and through numerous repetitions over the years, I have developed a decent repertoire of scriptures that can be relatively easily accessed by my memory, the Spirit, and even my computer. But even with computer retrieval systems (and of course I do rely upon mine a lot for scripture searches), if you don't have at least the general idea and a few key words to enter, you're not going to know what to look for.

You've got to "treasure it up in your mind" (D&C 84:85), and then it will be given to you, to draw out when you need it. "Treasure up" means to store up information and knowledge as you would something very valuable. This implies taking the time to apply the effective storage strategies suggested in this book for making these images clear, vivid, and easy for the Spirit to tap into when needed.

If you had a treasure you wouldn't want to store it in some dingy warehouse, where it could be easily lost. No, you would want to store it in a good safe place, with a tracking system, so it could be easily found when you needed it.

Now I'd like to share an example of how the Spirit can help. When I was mapping out what I wanted to include in this chapter, I was reminded of the statement I used at the beginning of the book about the apostles of old and their amazing ability to remember what they had seen and heard. I read that statement at least five years ago, and I couldn't remember where, although I thought it might have been from Hugh Nibley.

So I went to GospelLink, which contains Nibley's writings. However, I could not remember the wording. I didn't know if Brother Nibley referred to them as the apostles, the early church fathers, or what. And I couldn't recall if he described their abilities as amazing, phenomenal, or something else. So after no less than half a dozen searches, and poring through hundreds of wrong references, I gave up. Almost. I sat and I pondered. I had prayed before I started. It seemed that I might have read it in Nibley's book *Since Cumorah*, which sat on the shelf barely three feet from my elbow. I picked the book up and began to thumb through the table of contents when my wife called.

Someone was at the door for me. On my return, I thought, "Perhaps I'll have to find that quote later for another book. I'll just take one last look." So I opened the book, and there it was, halfway down, on the right side of the first page I opened to. Memories are marvelous, and computers are great, but neither can compare with the divine help that's available through the Spirit, if we first do our part.

But There's Never Enough Time

I am reminded of Jesus' gentle rebuke and comment to Martha regarding her workload and her sister Mary.

> "Now it came to pass, as they went, that he entered into a certain village: and a certain woman named Martha received him into her house.
>
> "And she had a sister called Mary, which also sat at Jesus' feet, and heard his word.
>
> "But Martha was cumbered about much serving, and came to him, and said, Lord, dost thou not care that my sister hath left me to serve alone? Bid her therefore that she help me.
>
> "And Jesus answered and said unto her, Martha, Martha, thou art careful and troubled about many things:
>
> "But one thing is needful: and Mary hath chosen that good part, which shall not be taken away from her." (Luke 10:38–42)

And so it is with the word of the Lord found in the scriptures. If we take time to pay close attention and vividly store them up in our memory, they will not be taken from us.

In that same fireside mentioned above, Elder Eyring went on to counsel, "There will be many instances when one thing crowds out another. But there should never be a conscious choice to let the spiritual become secondary as a pattern in our lives. Never. That will lead to tragedy. The tragedy may not be obvious at first, nor may it ever be clear in mortal life. But remember, you are interested in education not for life but for eternal life. When you see that reality clearly with spiritual sight, you will put spiritual learning first. . . .

"I cannot promise academic success or perfect families. Nor can I tell you the way in which He will honor His promise of adding blessings upon you. But I can promise you that if you will go to Him in prayer and ask what He would have you do next, promising that you will put His kingdom first, He will answer your prayer and He will keep His promise to add upon your head blessings, enough and to spare. Those apparent prison walls of 'not enough time' will begin to recede, even as you are called to do more."[9]

In Conclusion

I hope that the strategies I have shared have been encouraging, even exciting. I hope your mind has become energized with the possibilities for enhancing your capabilities to remember the scriptures, as well as the many other benefits that you and your loved ones can enjoy as a result of these increased abilities for retention and recall.

One observation: While these methods and ideas are proven to be effective, if you do not apply them you will lose the knowledge you could have retained had you persisted in applying them. I speak from experience here. As I've noted, I have used these off and on throughout my adult life. When I have, I've learned and retained in remembrance a knowledge of the scriptures that has been a great blessing to me, my family, and now, hopefully, you. But too often, I've felt I was too busy to take time to create vivid pictures or a few memorable links or pegs for better retention or retrieval.

As I've worked on this book, I've been haunted by what might have been if I had just taken a bit more time to apply these principles and methods more consistently in my life. What if I'd done just a little bit every day, every week, and so forth, worked up my game plan earlier, and been more persistent in my study and rehearsals? Think what a great wealth of wisdom I would now have to use in blessing the lives of others.

Learn from my oversight! Do not procrastinate your application of these lessons. We are talking about the word of the Lord, the iron rod, the bread of life, the riches of great wisdom, the words of salvation and eternal life, of which wise Solomon said, "All the things that may be desired are not to be compared to it" (Proverbs 8:11).

In Matthew 6, the Lord says, "Lay not up for yourselves treasures upon earth, where moth and rust doth corrupt, and where thieves break through and steal: But lay up for yourselves treasures in heaven, where neither moth nor rust doth corrupt, and where thieves do not break through nor steal" (Matthew 6:19–20).

This scripture often reminds me of the humorous but somewhat sobering story of the wealthy, righteous man who pleaded with God to be able to take some of his wealth with him when he died. Finally, one night an angel appeared and granted him his wish. He said he could take with him one briefcase and anything he could put into it. After much thought, the man reasoned that the item of greatest value for its size was gold. So he sold what he needed to fill his briefcase with gold bullion bars. Finally, the day came. As his mortal body failed him, he had tied to his wrist his very heavy briefcase. And when he died, true to the angel's words, he arrived on the other side with this suitcase still attached.

"Well," said St. Peter, "this is unusual." So the man explained about his request and the promise granted him. To which St. Peter replied, "Open it up. Let's see what valuable items you've brought." The man opened his briefcase and St. Peter exclaimed in dismay, "Pavement? You've brought pavement?"

I see two morals to that story. First, those things that are valued in heaven are probably quite different than what we value on earth. And second, the only things of value we can really take with us to the other side are those things that our spirits carry in our memories. Since wisdom and understanding were apparently highly valued before we came to earth (see Proverbs 8:23, 30), they will likely be held in high esteem hereafter as well. In fact Doctrine and Covenants 130:19 is quite explicit on that point. "And if a person gains more knowledge and intelligence in this life through his diligence and obedience than another, he will have so much the advantage in the world to come."

As noted in chapter 5, near-death studies seem to validate this point. Those who have returned often affirm that mortal life is a time to learn, gain experience, and grow in knowledge and in wisdom.

I pray that the principles, methods, and strategies that you have learned in this book will be of great value to you in that important endeavor. And if you will apply them, I believe they will. I think you will be amazed at the many blessings you will enjoy as a result throughout your period of probation here on the earth and in the world to come.

Notes

1. Hugh Nibley, *Since Cumorah*, 99.
2. Spencer W. Kimball, *The Teachings of Spencer W. Kimball*, 23.
3. Brigham Young, in *Journal of Discourses*, 4:22.
4. James E. Talmage, *Articles of Faith*, 147.
5. Joseph Fielding Smith, in Conference Report, October 1958, 21.
6. Joseph Fielding Smith, *Take Heed to Yourselves*, 364.
7. "The Greatest Gift," *Friend*, December 1977, 38.
8. Elder Henry B. Eyring, CES fireside for young adults, 6 May 2001.
9. Ibid.

APPENDIX

REMEMBERING THE TEN OPTIMIZING STRATEGIES

1. **Amplify the image**, making it longer, taller, bigger, fatter, and exaggerated.

2. **Create action.**

3. **See interaction** among the elements in your picture.

4. **Create unusual, outlandish, or unconventional** images or associations.

5. **See yourself in the scenes.**

For example, I see myself going over to our TV and adjusting the volume to *amplify* the sound. As I do this, the whole screen begins to *amplify*, or enlarge, until it reaches the ceiling—it's almost eight feet tall and twelve feet wide.

On the screen, I see a documentary on the filming of the *Ten Commandments*. The Israelites are poised on the banks of the Red Sea. I hear the director shout, "Action." Moses lifts his rod, the giant waves part, and all the people start running across the river bottom to the other side. They are followed by the chariots of Pharaoh.

However, before they can reach the Israelites, the elements (water) come crashing down, *interacting* with them—well, actually drowning them. Cecil B. DeMille says, "Wow, now that's great *interaction!*" He then sees a red speedboat traveling across the water and declares. "That's unusual. In fact, it's more than unconventional, it's outlandish! They didn't have those back in Moses' day!"

I then decide to get into the picture, so I dive into the tube. Next thing I know, I'm sitting in the boat skimming over the water and waving to DeMille on the bank. I can now really *see myself in the picture.*

6. **Use symbols** or easily pictured objects to represent common concepts.

7. **Develop and use *your own*** creative images and symbols.

8. **Draw pictures and symbols** to represent the concepts.

9. **Involve other senses (sound, touch, taste, and smell)** in your imagery.

10. **Read aloud, hear, and discuss.**

Back to our example. My speedboat finally comes to shore on the Israelites' side. As it does, I hear and then see the loud clashing of huge cymbals *(symbols)* announcing my arrival. I decide not to wait for DeMille; I'm going to *create my own pictures*. So I climb out of the boat, set up my easel, and begin *drawing pictures* and *symbols* representing this momentous occasion. As I'm doing so, I can *hear* the Israelites and their animals making all kinds of *noises*. Soon I can *smell* the burning of firewood as the children of Israel settle into camp.

My *other senses* pick up the action. I see the Israelites gathering together, so I go over to see what is happening. And I see and *hear* Moses *reading aloud* to them the promises of God from the record of Abraham.

Remembering the Books of the Old Testament

Here are the books of the Old Testament with the picture words I have developed and envisioned to help me link them in order, and peg their teaching to.

Exodus	Camel with items strapped to its back.
Leviticus	Levi jeans.
Numbers	Giant numbers large enough to stand on.
Deuteronomy	Moses and Aaron arm in arm as if singing a duet.
Joshua	Joshua from *The Ten Commandments*, the movie.
Judges	Two judges wearing black robes.
Ruth	A woman I know named Ruth.
1 Samuel	A man I know named Sam.
2 Samuel	The same Sam, although looking much older and with a beard.
1 Kings	A king with a crown.
2 Kings	Two kings joined at the back .
1 Chronicles	A newspaper, *The Daily Chronicle*,

rolled up.

2 Chronicles	Another newspaper, spread out.

Now to begin, I see a camel in a caravan (Exodus) with Levi jeans (Leviticus) on his hind legs, dragging a large number *36* (number of chapters in Numbers, with the top part of the *6* hooked to the bottom of the number *3*). Standing on the number *6* as it's being dragged along are Moses and Aaron, arm in arm, singing a duet (Deuteronomy). Aaron's left hand is stuck to Joshua's tar stick. Joshua (from the movie *The Ten Commandments)* is holding onto the other end of the stick; in his left hand, he has ahold of the black robes of two judges (Judges). A woman I know named Ruth has ahold of the second judge's black robes, which she uses to wipe her brow. Holding on to her left hand is a guy I know named Sam (1 Samuel). In his left hand, he has ahold of another, older man's beard. This man looks just like him only older and with a long white beard (2 Samuel). The old man carries a crown in his left hand, which belongs to the king in royal robes walking behind him (1 Kings). Stuck to the back of the first and walking backwards is another king (2 Kings), who has one newspaper (the *Daily Chronicle*) under his arm and is reading another (1 and 2 Chronicles).

Ezra	A sheriff who likes to take it easy (EZ).
Nehemiah	A man wearing a skirt hemmed at the knee.
Esther	A woman I know named Esther.
Job	An older bald guy.
Psalms	David playing a harp and singing.
Proverbs	Solomon with a white owl on his shoulder.
Ecclesiastes	Eggshells.
Song of Solomon	Solomon with a harp.

Isaiah	A British-looking chap with a pipe like the one Sherlock Holmes smokes, who likes to say, "I say, old boy."
Jeremiah	A man I know named Jerry.
Lamentations	An old man with a burlap sack filled with ashes, crying.
Ezekiel	A geeky-looking guy with wire-rimmed glasses taped at the corner and with pens in his pocket

Tied to the second King's waist is a sled and on it sits an older guy, named Ezra, sitting in an EZ chair. On the other end of the sled, a Scottish lad wearing a kilt is kneeling down (Nehemiah), and the hem of his skirt touches the ground. A woman named Esther is bent over and holding onto his ankles. An older, bald man with boils (Job) is wiping the secretions from the skin eruptions on his brow onto Esther's skirt. He's teetering on his right leg; his left leg is bent at the knee and is stuck behind him in David's harp (Psalms).

David is holding his son Solomon's white robe in his left hand. Solomon has a white owl on his left shoulder (Proverbs), but his left foot is stuck in a huge eggshell (Ecclesiastes), and he's holding a harp in his left hand (Song of Solomon). Sticking out of the harp is a big pipe held by a British chap who looks like Sherlock Holmes. After closely examining the harp, he declares into a megaphone, "I say, old boy, is this a real harp?" (Isaiah).

As the British gentleman bends over to look at the harp, my friend Jerry appears (Jeremiah). Now Jerry, a practical joker, places a firecracker in the older gentleman's back pocket. In Jerry's other hand, he's holding onto a burlap sack, owned by another older gentleman, who is sitting down, holding his head in his hands and crying (Lamentations). A geeky looking guy with old wire-rimmed glasses has his hand on the old man's left shoulder, trying to comfort him with some electronic device (Ezekiel).

Daniel	My friend Dan.
Hosea	A fireman with a hose in his hand.
Joel	My friend Joel.
Amos	A moss hanging from the trees.
Obadiah	A man wearing a black cowboy hat, looking like a bad guy from a Western— "Oh, bad guy."
Jonah	A man with a white, chalky appearance because he's been digested by a whale.
Micah	My cousin Mike.
Nahum	This prophet wears a nameplate with "Nahum" written on it.
Habakkuk	Has on his back a kettle for cooking.
Zephaniah	A girl named Stephanie wearing a zebra stripe.
Haggai	A man I know whose last name is Haggie; he also has a teddy bear named Huggie. (If you don't know a Haggie, perhaps you can think of someone who is always giving hugs.)
Zechariah	An elderly gentleman named Zeek, who cares.
Malachi	Has molasses on his kite.

Plugging in the geek's power cord and being shocked is my old friend Dan (Daniel), who is soaking because he's been sprayed by Hosea. Standing nearby, writing everything down on a soggy notepad is a newspaperman I know named Joel. Draped over Joel's back is a thick green moss (Amos), and tangled in the moss is the chin strap of a black cowboy hat, owned by a bad guy. How bad is he? "Oh, bad. Real bad." However, holding on to the black hat is a very white hand belonging to Jonah. On his head is a ball cap and in his left hand a mitt, owned and being pulled on by a guy I know named Mike, who likes baseball (Micah). Dangling from Mike's neck is a giant wooden nameplate (Nahum), and on his back he has a big kettle for cooking (Habakkuk).

Hugging the kettle is a girl I know named Stephanie, who also has a giant zebra stripe across her body, making her name Zephanie (Zephaniah); her hug reminds me of Haggai. To reinforce that, she is holding Huggie the teddy bear in her left hand. Tugging on the doll is an old Greek man named Zeek (Zachariah; he also has a Z stripe). In his left hand is a bad (mal) kite with molasses dripping off it (Malachi).

SOURCES

Allen, James. *As a Man Thinketh.* Salt Lake City: Bookcraft, 2002.

Best-Loved Poems of the LDS People. Edited by Jack M. Lyon, et al. Salt Lake City: Deseret Book, 1996.

Buzan, Tony. *The Mind Map Book: How to Use Radiant Thinking to Maximize Your Brain's Untapped Potential.* New York: Penguin Books, 1996.

———. *Use Both Sides of Your Brain.* New York: Penguin Books, 1991.

Cannon, George Q. *Gospel Truth: Discourses and Writings of President George Q. Cannon.* Edited by Jerreld L. Newquist. Salt Lake City: Deseret Book, 1987.

Conference Reports of The Church of Jesus Christ of Latter-day Saints. Salt Lake City: The Church of Jesus Christ of Latter-day Saints, 1898 to present.

Covey, Stephen R. *The Seven Habits of Highly Effective People.* New York: Simon & Schuster, 1989.

Crook, Thomas H., III, and Brenda D. Adderly. *The Memory Cure.* New York: Simon & Schuster, 1998.

Gaskill, Alonzo. *The Lost Language of Symbolism.* Salt Lake City: Deseret Book, 2003.

Grant, Heber J. *Gospel Standards.* Edited by G. Homer Durham. Salt Lake City: Improvement Era, 1941.

Higbee, Kenneth L. *Your Memory: How It Works and How to Improve It.* New York: Marlowe & Company, 1996.

Householder, Leslie. *Heavenly Help with Money Matters.* Mesa, Ariz.: ThoughtsAlive Books, 2005.

Journal of Discourses. 26 vols. London: Latter-day Saints' Book Depot, 1854–86.

Kimball, Spencer W. *The Teachings of Spencer W. Kimball.* Edited by Edward L. Kimball. Salt Lake City: Bookcraft, 1982.

Lapp, Danielle C. *Don't Forget.* Cambridge, Mass.: Perseus Books, 1995.

Lee, Harold B. *Stand Ye in Holy Places.* Salt Lake City: Deseret Book, 1974.

Leviton, Richard. *Brain Builders: A Lifelong Guide to Sharper Thinking, Better Memory, and an Age-Proof Mind.* Englewood Cliffs, N.J.: Prentice Hall, 1995.

Lewis, C. S. *The Screwtape Letters.* Rev. ed. New York: Macmillan, 1982.

Ley, Beth M. *Marvelous Memory Boosters.* Temecula, Calif.: BL Publications, 2000.

Lombard, Jay, and Carl Germano. *The Brain Wellness Plan: Breakthrough Medical, Nutritional, and Immune-Boosting Therapies.* New York: Kensington Publishing, 1997.

Ludlow, Victor L. *Isaiah: Prophet, Seer, and Poet.* Salt Lake City: Deseret Book, 1982.

Madsen, Truman G. *How to Stop Forgetting and Start Remembering—A Practical Digest.* Provo, Utah: T. G. Madsen, 1968.

Maxwell, Neal A. *Sermons Not Spoken.* Salt Lake City: Bookcraft, 1985.

Meichenbaum, Donald. *Cognitive-Behavior Modification: An Interactive Approach.* New York: Plenum Press, 1977.

Millet, Robert L. *Alive in Christ: The Miracle of Spiritual Rebirth.* Salt Lake City: Deseret Book, 1997.

Moody, Raymond. *The Light Beyond*. New York: Bantam Books, 1988.

Nelson, Aaron P., and Susan Gilbert. *The Harvard Medical School Guide to Achieving Optimal Memory*. New York: McGraw-Hill, 2005.

Nibley, Hugh. *Since Cumorah*. Salt Lake City: Deseret Book, 1967.

Ring, Kenneth. *Lessons from the Light*. New York: Insight Books, 1998.

Sahelian, Ray, and Karlis Ullis. *The Mind Boosters: Natural Supplements That Enhance Your Mind, Memory, and Mood*. New York: St. Martin's Press, 2000.

Smith, Joseph Fielding. *Take Heed to Yourselves*. Salt Lake City: Deseret Book, 1971.

Talmage, James. *The Articles of Faith*. Salt Lake City: Deseret Book, 1984.

We Believe: Doctrines and Principles of The Church of Jesus Christ of Latter-day Saints. Edited by Rulon T. Burton. Salt Lake City: Tabernacle Books, 1994.

Welch, John W. *Chiasmus in Antiquity*. Provo, Utah: Brigham Young University, 1981.

Whitaker, Julian. *The Memory Solution*. Garden City Park, N.Y.: Avery Publishing, 1999.

ABOUT THE AUTHOR

Born and raised on a family farm in Logan, Utah, David R. Larsen attended Utah State University on a track scholarship, majoring in education.

Following a mission to Argentina, three years in the army, and his marriage in Switzerland to Maureen Kulinicz, of Coventry, England, he returned to the states to complete his bachelor's degree in psychology at the University of Utah. He later received a master's degree in family and human development from Utah State University.

For seven years, he served as a chaplain in the U.S. Navy and Marine Corps and then as a Family Life Programs manager for the Air Force. In his career he has taught numerous classes, in both the United States and Europe, on marriage and family relations, as well as on organizational and individual development. Recently, he served as director of the Organizational Health and Consulting Office at Hill Air Force Base, in Ogden, Utah. David also serves on the Utah board of the International Association for Near-Death Studies (IANDS) and is currently the director of Advanced Memory Dynamics.

David and Maureen live in Layton, Utah. They have two children and four grandchildren.